GOD'S STORY

THE BIBLE EXPLAINED

MATT SEARLES

LION

Published by
Lion Hudson Limited
Wilkinson House, Jordan Hill Business Park
Banbury Road, Oxford OX2 8DR, England
www.lionhudson.com

ISBN (hardback) 978 0 74598 064 5
e-ISBN 978 0 74598 112 3

First edition 2021

Acknowledgments

Unless otherwise marked, Scripture quotations are taken from the Holy Bible, New International Version, copyright © 1973, 1978, 1984 International Bible Society. Used by permission of Hodder & Stoughton, a member of the Hodder Headline Group. All rights reserved. 'NIV' is a trademark of International Bible Society. UK trademark number 1448790.

Scripture quotations marked ESV are from The Holy Bible, English Standard Version® (ESV®) copyright © 2001 by Crossway, a publishing ministry of Good News Publishers. All rights reserved.

Scripture quotations marked KJV are taken from The Authorized (King James) Version. Rights in the Authorized Version are vested in the Crown. Reproduced by permission of the Crown's patentee, Cambridge University Press.

Scripture quotations marked NLT are taken from the Holy Bible, New Living Translation, copyright © 1996, 2004, 2007 by Tyndale House Foundation. Used by permission of Tyndale House Publishers, Inc., Carol Stream, Illinois 60188. All rights reserved.

Scripture quotations marked NRSV are from The New Revised Standard Version of the Bible copyright © 1989 by the Division of Christian Education of the National Council of Churches in the USA. Used by permission. All Rights Reserved.

Scripture quotations marked CSB are taken from the Christian Standard Bible. Copyright © 2017 by Holman Bible Publishers. Used by permission. Christian Standard Bible® and CSB® are federally registered trademarks of Holman Bible Publishers, all rights reserved.

Every effort has been made to trace copyright holders and to obtain permission for the use of copyright material. The publisher apologizes for any errors or omissions and would be grateful to be notified of any corrections that should be incorporated in future reprints of this book.

A catalogue record for this book is available from the British Library

Printed and bound in China, October 2020, LH54

CONTENTS

Introduction 5

1. The Bible: God Speaks 6

2. In the Beginning: God Created the World 8

3. Humanity: The Crown of Creation 11

4. A Royal Task: Fill and Subdue the Earth 14

5. The Fall: Sin Entered the World 17

6. Cast Out: Judgment and Salvation 19

7. The Flood: God's Covenant with Noah 21

8. Abraham: God's Gospel Promise 23

9. Covenant with Abraham: "I Will Be Your God" 25

10. Isaac, Jacob, and Joseph: Relentless Grace 28

11. Slaves in Egypt: Moses and Pharaoh 31

12. The Exodus: God Redeemed His People 34

13. Mount Sinai: The Law and the Covenant 37

14. The Tabernacle: God Dwells Among Us 40

15. Leviticus: Holiness, Priests, and Sacrifice 42

16. Numbers: Wilderness Wanderings 45

17. Deuteronomy: "Choose Life!" 48

18. Joshua: Entering the Promised Land 51

19. Judges: The Misery of Life with No King 54

20. Samuel: The Gift of Kingship 57

21. David: The Persecuted Messiah 60

22. Psalms: Prayers for All Seasons 63

23. Solomon: Prince of Peace 66

24. Wisdom Literature 1: The Order of Eden 69

25. Wisdom Literature 2: The Disorder of the Fall 72

26. The Kingdom Splits: God's Judgment Falls 75

27. Elijah and Elisha: God's Patience 78

28. The Exile: The Death of the Nation 80

29. The Prophets: God's Mouthpieces 83

30. Isaiah: Prophecy of a New Heavens and Earth 85

31. Jeremiah: Prophecy of a New Covenant 87

32. Ezekiel: Prophecy of a New Temple 90

33. Daniel and Esther: Living as Exiles 93

34. Ezra and Nehemiah: The Return from Exile 96

35. Minor Prophets: Darkness Before the Dawn 99

36. Jesus: Who is This Man? 102

37. Four Gospels: Portraits of Jesus 105

38. Jesus' Birth: Heaven Embraced Earth 108

39. Jesus' Early Ministry: The Coming of the Lord 111

40. Jesus' Teaching: Gospel and Kingdom 114

41. Jesus' Miracles: Signs of a Restored World 117

42. Disciples and Opponents: Jesus' Identity 120

43. Jesus' Final Days: Ministry in Jerusalem 122

44. The Last Supper: Preparing for the End 125

45. The Cross: The Centre of the Bible's Story 128

46. The Resurrection: New Creation Begun 131

47. Pentecost: God Sends His Spirit 134

48. Acts: Jesus' Mission Continues 137

49. Paul: Witness of the Resurrected Christ 139

50. Paul's Theology: Justification by Faith 142

51. Paul's Theology: Union with Christ 145

52. Christian Living in the Last Days: Tension 148

53. The Church: God's Plan for the World 151

54. Father, Son, and Spirit: The Trinity 154

55. The Return of Christ: The Day of Justice 157

56. The End of All Things: The New Creation 160

Notes 163

Glossary 164

Picture credits 167

INTRODUCTION

According to *Time* magazine, "the Bible is the most influential book ever written"[1]. However, as a collection of sixty-six books, written by multiple authors, over many centuries it can feel hard to access. Many wonder if it has an overarching message. Many are unsure about where to begin. Reading cover to cover is a daunting prospect. But starting in the middle feels like being dropped into unfamiliar country with no map and little understanding of the landmarks.

This book will set out how the Bible is one unified whole, with one coherent plot. The Bible's story is the backbone on which everything else hangs. If it is in place, everything else works properly. Or, to pick up the previous metaphor, the Bible story is like the map of this unfamiliar country. Each individual part of the Bible makes sense in light of the whole.

This book is written assuming no prior knowledge, so will be suitable for someone who is not a Christian but who wants to learn about the Bible or the Christian faith. But by setting out the main story of the Bible, this book will also appeal to those who may have been Christians for years but have never quite seen how the whole Bible hangs together. Terms that may be unfamiliar are explained in the glossary at the back of this book.

Because the Bible is a story, a good way to read this book is from the beginning, seeing how the plot develops. But each unit is self contained, so feel free to dip in where you like.

Like all good stories, the Bible story has conflict. There are not just heroes and villains, but complex characters. There are stories of rags-to-riches, of great falls from grace, of quests completed, and others only barely begun. The tapestry is vast, taking in the rise and fall of nations, but there is attention given to individuals too: the book of Ruth recounts the story of a refugee widow and her future husband during one short harvest season. At the heart of the story is Jesus Christ, presented by the Bible as God himself come to earth, setting aside his power and embracing weakness.

Peter Wilby, the atheist newspaper editor, wrote one Christmas of how this story intrigued him:

All religions have stories at their heart. Christianity, to my mind, has the best: an omnipotent God who chooses to be incarnated as a human, born in the most humble circumstances imaginable. Whether or not we are believers, we should all celebrate that story in the coming days and ponder its meaning.[2]

I hope this book will help you get an idea of this astonishing story, and ponder its meaning. For Christians, the Bible is not just *a* story, it is *the* story – the story of the whole world.

THE BIBLE: GOD SPEAKS

How could small finite creatures know a vast infinite God? They could not – unless he chose to reveal himself in ways they could understand. The Bible presents itself as just such a revelation. Not humanity's thoughts *about* God, but a personal address *from* God. God speaking so that people can know him, can have a relationship with him.

The story in miniature

The Bible is one coherent whole, telling the story of God's plan to save the world through Jesus Christ. Though it is vast in scope, with different authors and an astonishing array of characters and sub-plots, it still has a very basic structure, shared by all good stories:

The setting	Creation **Genesis 1–2**	God created a beautiful world with a paradise garden where he would live with humanity. Humanity is tasked with making the world more glorious.
The conflict	The Fall **Genesis 3–11**	Satan (the serpent) tempts humanity to disobey God, leading them to be cast out of the garden and unable to complete their mission.
The rising action	Redemption **Genesis 12 –** **Revelation 20**	God made promises to Abraham to restore all things through his family. Abraham's family became a nation, and were given a land where they would know God's blessing. But then they sinned and were cast out of the land – things looked worse than ever.
		Jesus came to relive the story of Israel. He is the descendant of Abraham who would bring blessing. The story climaxes in Jesus' death and resurrection – one of the great reversals in literary history. This seeming defeat was in fact Jesus' greatest victory. He conquered Satan and death, so his people could re-enter the presence of God.
The conclusion	Consummation **Revelation 21–22**	The goal has been reached, the conflict overcome, and the villain defeated. God's people live with him in a newly created paradise, more glorious even than the first creation. Jesus, the hero of the whole story, is vindicated, honoured, and marries his bride – his people – in a perfect happy ending.

Jonah being swallowed by a fish. An illustration from the Kennicott Bible of 1476

The books of the Bible

THE OLD TESTAMENT – thirty-nine books written mainly in Hebrew	THE NEW TESTAMENT – twenty-seven books written in Greek
History Genesis to Esther	**Gospels** (Matthew, Mark, Luke, John)
Poetry Job to Song of Songs	**Acts of the Apostles**
Prophecy Isaiah to Malachi	**Letters** Romans – Jude
	Revelation

The simplest way to think of the relationship between the Old and New Testament is that of promise and fulfilment. The Old Testament story is incomplete on its own. The New Testament completes the story, and shows the true fulfilment of all promises made in the Old Testament. Despite there being sixty-six books and many different authors, Christians believe the Bible to be one book, with one coherent story, because the ultimate author of the Bible is God himself, who inspired each human author in what they wrote (2 Peter 1:21).

How to understand the Bible

Reading the Bible can seem daunting. Three key principles make the task much easier (and are the principles that underpin the approach of this book).

1. **Read later scripture in light of what precedes it.** The biblical authors deliberately developed the existing story, using similar language and themes. The most helpful background for understanding Mark's Gospel (for example) is not history or archeology, but the Old Testament, primarily the prophecies of Isaiah. This book will seek to draw out some of these links, with regular "Old Testament fulfilment" sections in the New Testament part of this book.

2. **Read in light of Christ.** Jesus said that the Old Testament testified about him (John 5:39). The Bible is about God before it is about us. So don't read it just looking for moral examples or lessons for today. First, try to see how what you're reading forms part of the story climaxing in Jesus. In the Old Testament part of this book there are regular "Looking ahead to Jesus" sections.

3. **Read in light of the main story.** It can be easy to get lost in the details of the Bible. Keep an eye on the main story: God's plan to restore all things through Jesus Christ. This introductory book cannot cover every detail and much must be left out, but we will focus on the main story that makes sense of everything else.

IN THE BEGINNING: GOD CREATED THE WORLD

In the beginning, God spoke, and a world came to be. Seas and oceans, mountains and valleys, lions and eagles, ants and starfish, all created by God's powerful word. All of creation reverberates with the joy of its creator, and reflects – in some small part – the beauty and generosity of the God who authored it. No wonder that as God laid the foundations of the earth "the morning stars sang together and the angels shouted for joy" (Job 38:7).

"And God said..."

Other ancient accounts of creation (from Babylon, Egypt, and Greece) describe struggles between various gods; in contrast the account in Genesis 1–2 emphasizes God's power, authority, and goodness. He created simply by *speaking*. With just a word, galaxies were born, the heavens were stretched out like a tent, and all beasts and creatures sprang into life. Everything that exists only does so because God spoke it into existence. Scripture consistently describes God as a speaking God, and emphasizes the power of his words.

> By the word of the LORD the
> heavens were made,
>   their starry host by the breath of
> his mouth.

Psalm 33:6

The spectacular Northern Lights

Forming and filling

Genesis chapter 1 presents a very ordered account, with the six days of creation in matching pairs. On the first three days, God creates the universe as a "house" with three different environments. On the next three days, God populates each of these environments in turn.

FORMING	FILLING
Day 1: "Let there be light." God separated the light from darkness and made day and night.	**Day 4:** God made the sun and the moon to govern the day and night, and mark the seasons. He also made the stars.
Day 2: God separated the waters above from the waters below and made the sky.	**Day 5:** God created the birds of the sky and the creatures of the sea.
Day 3: God gathered the seas and made the dry land, and caused vegetation to grow.	**Day 6:** God made the living creatures to live on the land, and then made humanity.

"It was good"

A repeated refrain runs throughout Genesis 1: "And God saw that it was good." When God had finished creating and saw all that he had made, he pronounced it *very* good. This has profound implications for a Christian view of the physical world, and indeed of God himself.

The ancient Greeks believed that the physical world was inferior to spiritual realities, as do many religions and philosophies today. They viewed material things as unimportant, or even evil. Yet God's verdict "it was good" means that families and society, music and zoology, sunsets and coffee are all part of God's good creation, to be valued and enjoyed to the glory of God. There is no division between the "sacred" and the "secular". Everything God made is good, and is to be enjoyed and received with thanksgiving.

God's pronouncement of "it was good" also means that creation reveals something about God. The picture we receive in Genesis 1 is not of a God who gives simply the minimum – in fact he gives extravagantly! Creation is a generous gift, given by a generous creator. The world is

The Soweto Gospel Choir – a vibrant reminder that we are physical beings, created to sing and dance and enjoy the bodies God has given us

rich with possibilities, with wonder, with beauty. God didn't need to make the world so intricate, curious, and mysterious. But he wanted to. The Bible is clear that this good world has been spoiled by sin (as we shall see in later chapters), but nonetheless, it still gleams with fragments of beauty, every one a fingerprint of the God who made it.

The Earth from space

I had the intention of becoming a theologian... but now I see how God is, by my endeavours, also glorified in astronomy, for "the heavens declare the glory of God".

Johannes Kepler (1571–1630), scientist who discovered the laws of planetary motion

The theology of creation

Christians differ on whether the "days" spoken of refer to literal 24-hour periods, or much longer, but all agree that this is not a "scientific" account, trying to answer the question *how* it was made. Rather this account answers the *who?* question. *God* made it. The world has a beginning, but God has no beginning. He has always existed: Father, Son, and Spirit in perfect relationship (see p. 154, the Trinity). God is *creator* – creator of *all* things, seen and unseen. This has profound consequences:

- God is the rightful ruler of creation and all that is in it. He made it, so he owns it.
- The things of creation derive their meaning from God. His word explains creation.
- God is different from creation. He is not to be thought of as being like his creatures. Theologians call this the "Creator–creature" distinction.

LOOKING AHEAD TO JESUS:
Author of creation

Although Jesus is not explicitly mentioned until much later in the Bible, he is present right at the start. Speaking of Jesus, Paul says "all things have been created through him and for him. He is before all things, and in him all things hold together" (Colossians 1:16–17). Not only is Jesus the one through whom God the Father created the world, he is also the one for whom the world was created. Jesus is the answer to the question "Why is there something rather than nothing?" Jesus rejoices in the world; it brings him pleasure (Proverbs 8:31). The question is: how will Jesus use this world that he owns? What are his purposes for it? These are the questions that the rest of the story will answer.

HUMANITY: THE CROWN OF CREATION

What is it to be human? Are we simply naked apes? Are we just an animal like any other – albeit the species that happens to be dominant on earth at present? Or are we more than this? Instinctively we feel that human beings are valuable, and have dignity. We even dare to speak of *purpose*, beyond simple procreation. The Genesis account points to the reason we believe humans to have this meaning and worth. Humanity has been made *different* to the rest of creation.

In the image of God

So God created mankind in his own image,
in the image of God he created them;
male and female he created them.

Genesis 1:27

The statue of Horus at Edfu

In the ancient world, kings would place statues or images of themselves around their empire to represent their rule. In a similar way, ancient temples would have at their heart a statue of the god who was worshipped there, representing something of what that god was like.

When the God of the Bible wanted to show the world what he was like he didn't make a lifeless statue, rather he created humanity "in his image". Humans were made to reflect something of God's character, and were supposed to communicate and display that to the world. Thus there are two related aspects to being in God's image:

Being "in God's image" means that all humans have great worth and dignity regardless of their age, sex, or ethnic background. Rich or poor, educated or illiterate, able bodied or disabled, born or unborn – all humans are valuable. This is not value given by the particular society one lives in and dependent on the contribution one can make, but value given by God himself.

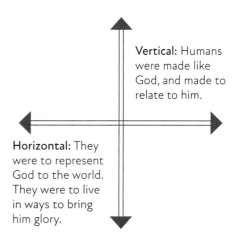

Vertical: Humans were made like God, and made to relate to him.

Horizontal: They were to represent God to the world. They were to live in ways to bring him glory.

Michaelangelo's *Creation of Adam*

The Garden of Eden

God planted a garden in the east, in Eden. Later this will be described as being on top of a mountain (Ezekiel 28:13–14), and from this mountain garden, a river flowed out to the rest of the earth. God planted the garden with trees that were pleasing to the eye and good for food (Genesis 2:9). In the middle of the garden were two special trees: the tree of life and the tree of the knowledge of good and evil. God placed the man in the garden, or, more literally, he "rested" the man in the garden. Adam, the first man, was permitted to eat the fruit from all the trees, apart from the tree of the knowledge of good and evil (Genesis 2:17).

Male and female he created them

Initially God just made Adam, but the first thing in all of creation that is pronounced "not good" is the fact that the man is on his own. The problem is not primarily loneliness, but rather that the task Adam has been given is not one he can complete on his own. On his own he can't fill the earth and subdue it (see p. 14). On his own he can't be the image of God to the world. The woman Eve is created as a "suitable helper" for Adam. This has no connotation of inferiority, but rather of complementarity. Elsewhere God himself will be described as the helper of Israel (Psalm 33:20), and he is certainly not inferior to humanity. Adam and Eve are created with equal dignity, in the image of God. Already, this points ahead to the fact that God is Trinity (see p. 154), that he can only be represented by humans in *relationship*. Adam sings a love song to Eve, and this is the first marriage and the first sexual relationship in the Bible. It is a beautiful picture of intimacy and companionship.

The seventh day: Rest

God created in six days, but the goal of creation is seen in the seventh: "God blessed the seventh day and

The union of man and woman in marriage

made it holy, because on it he rested from all the work of creating that he had done" (Genesis 2:3). This "rest" ("sabbath" in the original Hebrew) was a time for God and humanity to enjoy relationship in the good world that God had created. This is the goal of creation: that humans might enjoy relationship with God himself, with all the joy, peace, and contentment this brings. The greatest gift to humanity was not the creation – wonderful though it was – but God himself.

This idyllic picture of paradise with God would not last long. Because of human sin, this rest enjoyed in the Garden of Eden would be a distant memory. But millennia later, Jesus would come to restore all that was broken. He said, "Come to me, all you who are weary and burdened, and I will give you rest" (Matthew 11:28). His people can know rest with him in this age, but also the greater "rest" in the new creation to come.

LOOKING AHEAD TO JESUS:
The perfect bridegroom
There are many parallels between the first two chapters of the Bible and the last two. One of these is that the story begins and ends with a wedding. Genesis records the marriage between Adam and Eve is a pointer to a greater marriage; Revelation 21 and 22 describe the love and unity and commitment between Jesus Christ and his people in terms of a marriage. At its heart, the Bible is a romance.

A ROYAL TASK: FILL AND SUBDUE THE EARTH

Adam and Eve were placed in a garden, but they were given a world. From the mountain of Eden, they were to follow the rivers to distant seas and far-off shores. They were to fill and subdue, protect and cultivate, as they populated the world with children, transformed wilderness into orchards, dug out gold and jewels, discovered coffee, chocolate, and saffron. They had a job to do, a mission to complete, a world to beautify...

A royal task

It is sometimes said that Adam and Eve only had one rule: don't eat from the forbidden tree. But there were positive commands as well: be fruitful and increase in number. Fill the earth and subdue it. Rule over all the creatures. Work and keep the garden. The way these commands are introduced is very significant: "God *blessed* them and said..." (Genesis 1:28, emphasis added). The task God gave Adam and Eve was an extraordinary privilege and blessing. This was a royal task: to rule. Being in God's image, Adam and Eve were to rule the world under his authority.

A perfect world?

The world God created was very good, but it was not yet as glorious as it could be. For the world to flourish, someone was needed to work the ground (Genesis 2:5). The trees that produced fruit could also produce wood for fire or for making musical instruments. The sand that lay strewn across beaches would one day be stained glass windows, and silicon chips powering computers. The jewels buried deep in the earth would one day adorn the Temple (see p. 67) and be given to lovers with fire in their eyes. God gave Adam and Eve – and the children they would have – the astonishing privilege of bringing the world from one degree of glory to another. As one author comments:

> The world that God handed over to Adam and Eve was not a dusty museum that needed to be preserved exactly as it was for millennia to come. No, it was an art gallery full of beautiful white canvases waiting to be made even more beautiful by hundreds of mini-artists created in the Great Artist's image.[3]

At its best, human development is meant to bring the world to greater glory and beauty

A luscious green garden brings to mind the place of paradise where Adam and Eve met with God

The trees that God planted were "pleasing to the eye and good for food" (Genesis 2:9), and human culture should also value beauty as well as usefulness. Painting and pottery, industry and innovation – all were given by God to make the world even more glorious.

Expanding the boundaries of Eden

The Garden of Eden was the place of paradise where Adam and Eve met with God. It is deliberately described in similar terms to the Temple, which would be the dwelling place of God many years later (see table). Adam and Eve were to "work and take care of" (or protect) the garden, preserving the sanctity of this holy place (Genesis 2:15). But they were not to spend all of their time there. They were also to go out and fill and subdue the earth. They were to make the world like the garden. They were to expand the boundaries of Eden so that the whole earth would become a glorious temple, where God would be glorified amongst his people.

Correspondences between the Garden of Eden and the tabernacle/Temple

GARDEN OF EDEN	TABERNACLE/TEMPLE
Paradise with beautiful trees and flowers.	Decorated to look like gardens, with almond trees and blossoms, palm trees, pomegranates.
Gold and precious stones are found there (Genesis 2:11–12).	Gold and precious stones are used in decoration (Exodus 25:7, 11, 17, 31).
Adam is to "work and keep the garden" (Genesis 2:15).	The only other reference to "work and keep" in the Pentateuch is when referring to priests in the tabernacle (Numbers 3:7–8; 8:26; 18:5–6).
Dwelling place of God. God "walks" with his people in the Garden (Genesis 3:8).	Dwelling place of God (Exodus 25:8). God "walks" in the Temple (Leviticus 26:11–12).
Entered from the East and guarded by cherubim (Genesis 3:24).	Entered from the East. Cherubim embroidered on the curtain keeping people out of the Holy of Holies (Exodus 26:31).
Eden was a mountain (Ezekiel 28:13–14).	Mountains as places where people met with God: Mount Sinai, then the Temple.
Rivers flowed out from the Eden, giving life to the world (Genesis 2:10–14).	Life-giving river flows from the new Temple in Ezekiel (Ezekiel 47:1–12).

Going deeper: A covenant with Adam?

What would have happened if Adam hadn't eaten from the forbidden tree? What if he had obeyed? Many have seen God's relationship with Adam as a "covenant" (Hosea 6:7). A covenant is a binding agreement with obligations. Keeping the covenant leads to blessings, breaking it leads to curses. For Adam, the conditions are that he must fill and subdue the earth, and not eat from the forbidden tree. If he disobeyed, he would die. But what about the other side? What if he had obeyed? What blessings would he have received? First, he would have kept on eating from the tree of life, and so lived forever. Second, he would also have grown in maturity, eventually becoming not simply sinless, but *unable* to sin.

This covenant was dependent on perfect obedience. It was a covenant of "works". Adam's response to this covenant would determine the direction of the rest of human history. Would he obey and live – indeed grow into a greater quality of life? Or would he rebel and die?

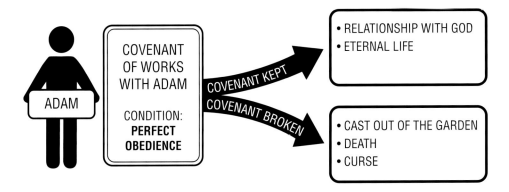

LOOKING AHEAD TO JESUS:
The second Adam

Adam had a representative role. His obedience, or his sin, would have consequences for the entire human race. Jesus came as the "second Adam" – a second representative figure who would hold the destiny of all humanity. This is why it is important to understand Adam. Jesus came not simply to deal with the sin that Adam brought into the world (see p. 17) but also to obey in the way that Adam should have. Jesus would fulfil God's original creation plans: he would rule it rightly, fill the earth with God's glory, and in doing so would bring blessing to all his people.

THE FALL: SIN ENTERED THE WORLD

The world is a beautiful place, full of wonder. But there is also brokenness and pain. Sorrow lurks in the dark corners of the world and of our hearts. Things are not *as they should be*. Genesis 3 is the first great turning point in the Bible story, and explains why this is the case. Until now, everything has been good. Adam and Eve had a garden–sanctuary to enjoy, a world to explore and subdue. Yet a small voice said that that was not enough…

"Did God really say… ?"

A serpent appears on the scene. Here it is simply described as "crafty", but later Scripture will identify this serpent with Satan (see "The origin of evil" below). The serpent does nothing more than speak to Eve, but its deceptive words twist and manipulate, aiming to lead Adam and Eve to disobey God and eat from the Tree of the Knowledge of Good and Evil – the one tree that has been forbidden. As we can see below, the serpent questions and twists God's words.

SERPENT'S WORDS (GENESIS 3:1–5)	WHAT THE SERPENT IS DOING
"Did God really say… ?"	Questioning God's word.
"Did God really say you must not eat from any tree in the garden?"	Questioning God's generosity. The serpent makes God seem restrictive – actually God had said they could eat from *all* trees apart from one.
"You will not surely die."	Questioning God's judgment.

Eve being tempted by the serpent in the Garden of Eden, from a window in Notre Dame Cathedral, Paris

You will be like God, knowing good and evil

The serpent also says that God has forbidden this tree because when they ate of it they would become like God, knowing good and evil (Genesis 3:5).

The irony should not be lost here. Adam and Eve have been created "in the image of God". They already are like God. And here is this creature, who is not made in God's image, telling them to follow his words to become more like God.

The promise of knowing good and evil may indicate more than simply knowing about good and evil, but may have a sense of deciding what is good and evil – being in a position like God. Adam and Eve do gain a "knowledge" through eating of this tree, but it is not knowledge that is good for them; rather they become aware of their nakedness. And they don't become more like God; rather they become less like him, with all the sorrow that that entails.

How should Eve have responded?

Adam (and by implication Eve) had been put in the garden to work it and take care of it – as seen on p. 15, this "taking care" has the sense of *protecting*. Part of Adam and Eve's role was to protect the garden from unclean serpents like this. They should have either killed the serpent, or at least cast it out of the garden.

But instead, Eve looked at the tree of the knowledge of good and evil and saw that its fruit was "good for food and pleasing to the eye" as well as being desirable for gaining wisdom. In fact, all the other trees in the garden were described as "good for food and pleasing to the eye", but her eyes were taken off all the good gifts that God had generously given, to the one thing that was not permitted. So she ate, and she gave some fruit to Adam, who ate also.

The serpent is traditionally identified with Satan

The origin of evil

Where did the snake come from? It appears on the scene with no real introduction. The text doesn't address this question directly, but two things are clear:

Satan is not a rival god. There are only two types of thing in the world: created things, and God the creator. Satan and evil are part of the world of created things. The Bible does not present good and evil in a power struggle – a view known as dualism. Rather the Bible presents God as utterly sovereign – in control of all events. Satan can't attack God himself, which is why he attacks God's people on earth.

God is not responsible for evil. When God created, consistently he pronounced his verdict as "good". God made a *good* creation, with no evil and no defect in it. Elsewhere we read of Satan as a *fallen* angel – a being who was created good, but who sought equality with God, and who turned from good to evil (2 Peter 2:4).

LOOKING AHEAD TO JESUS:
Dealing with evil

The Bible is less interested in answering the question "Where did evil come from?" than the question, "'What is God going to do about it?" This is what drives the rest of the story of Scripture.

The question of evil can only truly be answered by looking at Jesus. In Jesus, God's intentions are clearly made known: he is good, and he opposes evil. More than that, in Jesus God demonstrates the lengths he will go to destroy evil, to bring justice, and to bless his people: he will even be prepared to die to make it happen.

Adam and Eve by Lucas Cranach the Elder, 1526

CAST OUT: JUDGMENT AND SALVATION

Adam and Eve had sinned. They had rebelled against God, and eaten from the one forbidden tree. They knew that the punishment they deserved was death. So much promise, so much expectation, yet all seems now about to be dashed, the story over before it's even really begun. Yet even in the darkest of places, hope shines forth...

The results of sin

Sin had offered so much: being like God; knowing good and evil. Yet rather than bring freedom and satisfaction it brought insecurity and shame. Adam and Eve covered themselves with fig leaves, no longer happy to be seen in their nakedness. They heard the Lord walking in the garden in the cool of the day, and rather than go to him they hid. They were afraid.

The Lord judged Adam and Eve. They, and the whole human race that followed them, would live under the shadow of death. They would be cast from the garden – the place of life and peace – and live in a world of conflict.

Adam and Eve are cast out of Eden, from a window in Saint Aignan Church, Chartres

Conflict with the world

God said that the woman would face pain in childbirth. There would be greater difficulty in the task of filling the earth (see p. 14). This theme of pain and danger in childbirth, as well as barrenness and infertility, is a dominant one in the rest of Genesis.

The ground is cursed, so that it produces thorns and thistles. Not only will it take great effort and toil to get food, but also the task of ruling over creation will become much harder. Work was a good gift of God in creation, but since the fall, work will always be bound up with frustration. Also, creation is no longer as it should be. There are famines, natural disasters, diseases. All these result from Adam's sin, and the fact that creation has now been subjected to frustration and decay (Romans 8:20–21).

Conflict with each other

The woman is told, "Your desire will be for your husband and he will rule over you" (Genesis 3:16). The words "desire" and "rule" here have negative connotations, speaking of hostility between Adam and Eve. Again, this is directly related to the commission they received. Only together could they "fill the earth", but this hostility threatens that. Although this judgment is primarily on the marriage relationship, this hostility will also be seen in all human relationships: in the very next chapter their son Cain kills his brother Abel, and power struggles and rivalries have characterized human relationships since then.

Conflict with God

The most fundamental broken relationship is that with God. Adam and Eve were banished from the Garden of Eden, the place of relationship with God. No longer would they walk with God in the

The curse brought about through Adam and Eve's sin would be reversed by an offspring of the woman: Jesus. *Virgin Mary and Eve* by Sister Grace Remington

Thorns and thistles reflect the consequences on nature of Adam and Eve's sin

garden in the cool of the day. No longer would they have access to his presence, or be able to eat from his tree of life. Previously Adam and Eve were to guard the garden against evil, but after they were cast out, cherubim – mighty angels – were placed on the east side of the garden as guardians to prevent *them* coming back in.

Hope: The serpent-crusher

The clearest beacon of hope in this chapter – one that shines undimmed through even the darkest times of the rest of the story – is found in the curse the Lord pronounces upon the serpent:

And I will put enmity
between you and the woman,
and between your offspring and hers;
he will crush your head,
and you will strike his heel.

Genesis 3:15

There will be a conflict between the offspring of the serpent and the offspring of the woman – referring to the conflict between Satan and all of God's people that will continue for all the Bible story. But the end of the verse speaks of one *single* offspring of the woman, who will be struck by the serpent, but who will crush the serpent's head and defeat evil forever.

A number of figures in the Old Testament partially fulfil this role, for example Moses, Joshua, David. But the true serpent-crusher is Jesus Christ. He was struck by Satan, but through his death achieved the once-for-all defeat of evil that the world so badly needed.

LOOKING AHEAD TO JESUS:
Clothed in animal skins

Because of their sin, Adam and Eve are left hiding in shame at their nakedness. But as they are cast out of the garden, the Lord clothes them in animal skins, replacing the fig leaves they had been trying to cover themselves with (Genesis 3:21). This is not yet the royal robes that befit Adam and Eve as royal figures. But it points to God's provision. An innocent animal died so that they could be covered. In this act there is a foreshadowing of Jesus: an innocent victim who suffered – suffered the nakedness and shame of death on a cross – so that his people might be clothed and have their sin and shame covered.

07 THE FLOOD: GOD'S COVENANT WITH NOAH

Genesis chapters 4–11 make gloomy reading. Cain killed his brother Abel out of jealousy. The second murder follows quickly after. People have thrown off the shackles and are living free from God's laws, but the result is not freedom, but misery. Genesis 5 is a family tree, but the telling part of it is the repeated refrain "and he died". Life east of Eden is one of conflict, and the shadow of death hangs over everyone. Not only is there no sign of a faithful "serpent-crusher", but each generation gets more wicked than the last and humanity seems in a downward spiral. It seems as if the serpent's plans, rather than God's, are being fulfilled.

The flood

The Lord was grieved when he saw the wickedness of humanity, and he even regretted that he had made them. He determined to punish their wickedness with a flood, to wipe them from the face of the earth. Only Noah and his family were righteous, and so God told Noah to build an ark to save them from the floodwaters. So follows the familiar story of the building of the ark, the animals going in two by two, and the forty days and nights of rain. Noah and his family – along with the animals – were saved, but everything else on the face of the earth was destroyed. Despite being familiar as a children's story, this is a tragic and horrific tale: almost all of humanity destroyed because of their wickedness. At creation God separated the waters from the land, but now this is reversed, and the flood is an act of de-creation.

The dove returns to the Ark with an olive branch, from the Winchester Bible

God's covenant with Noah

When Noah and his family left the ark, they had to start afresh. God made a covenant with Noah, using almost identical language to that with Adam. Noah was told to "be fruitful and multiply" (Genesis 9:1, ESV). He was told to fill the earth, and was given dominion over the creatures. He was ruler over a sort of new creation, and he is presented as a new Adam figure. God hadn't abandoned his original creation plans. The judgment of the flood – horrific as it was – was not an end in itself, but a means towards the greater goal of God's creation plans being fulfilled.

Perhaps, then, Noah is the obedient Adam we have been waiting for. Perhaps he is the "offspring of the woman" who will crush wickedness forever. Perhaps he is the one who will give "rest" (which is what the name "Noah" means) to God's people like in the Garden of Eden.

Sadly, though, Noah got drunk. He then sinned, just like Adam. Noah was not the new Adam humanity needed. God's covenant with Noah affirms God's continuing creation purposes. God still intends a man to rule over the earth and God still intends for his presence and glory to expand to fill the entire earth. God hasn't given up on humanity.

The covenant of preservation

The distinctive feature of the covenant with Noah is *preservation*. God promised Noah that he would not flood the earth again. This is visually symbolized by the rainbow. The word is that used of a battle-bow. In the flood, God's battle-bow was pointed at the earth in judgment. God's covenant with Noah takes that bow and hangs it in the sky: a weapon of war has now become a beautiful symbol of peace. God's solution to human sinfulness is not to keep wiping out the wicked. Humanity doesn't need a

A rainbow symbolizes God's covenant with Noah

new start; humanity needs a new *heart*. The flood didn't provide this, but God's covenant with Noah gave more *time*. As has been commented, "The covenant made with Noah creates a firm stage of history where God can work out his plan for rescuing his fallen world."[4]

Babel: Increasing wickedness

Following the story of Noah is the story of the tower of Babel. Rather than filling the earth and bringing God glory – as humanity was created to do (see p. 14) – instead they gather together in one place and build a tower to make a name for *themselves*. It is really an attempt to regain Eden, to climb back up to paradise on their own terms, and be like God himself. The Lord came down in judgment and scattered the peoples, mixing up their languages so they would not understand one another.

Even after the flood, humanity is as wicked as ever. The tension is set up: how can God keep his promises – which are dependent on an obedient humanity – when humanity is so incapable of doing anything other than following their father Adam into sin and rebellion? Against this dark backdrop of Babel, God's light of grace would shine afresh, all beginning with promises made to Abraham...

LOOKING AHEAD TO JESUS:
Salvation through judgment

The story of Noah's ark is a vivid picture of salvation through judgment.[5] Against the dark and stormy background of God's judgment, Noah and his family had to trust God's appointed means of rescue. In the New Testament, the apostle Peter draws on this image to speak of the salvation Jesus offers (1 Peter 3:18–22). People today can be saved from the overwhelming flood of final judgment by trusting in Christ and the salvation he provides.

The Tower of Babel by Pieter Bruegel the Elder

ABRAHAM: GOD'S GOSPEL PROMISE

Things were bleak. Even after the flood, human wickedness continued to increase and God's creation promises seemed a distant memory. God's promise of an "offspring" who would put things right still remained, but people had come and gone and there was still no sign; rather the offspring of the serpent seemed to be running rampant. And so when we meet Abraham and Sarah, who had no children, we think this is the last we'll hear of them. How could a childless couple be the ones to provide the "offspring" the world needs? Nor do they have great spiritual credentials – they were worshippers of other gods (Joshua 24:2). They are no-hopers. But it is the glory of God to give hope where there is none, to give blessing in the most unlikely circumstances, to bring creation from nothing.

The great turning point

God's promise to Abraham in Genesis 12:1–3 is the great turning point in the Bible. Prominent church leader John Stott put it this way: "It may truly be said without exaggeration that not only the rest of the Old Testament but the whole of the New Testament are an outworking of these promises of God."[6]

Go from your country, your people and your father's household to the land I will show you.

I will make you into a great nation,
  and I will bless you;
I will make your name great,
  and you will be a blessing.
I will bless those who bless you,
  and whoever curses you I will curse;
and all peoples on earth
  will be blessed through you.

Genesis 12:1–3

Abraham was called to leave his homeland and travel to the land of Canaan

Land, offspring, blessing

There are three primary aspects to what God promises Abraham: people, land, and blessing.

PROMISE TO ABRAHAM	WHAT GOD WILL DO	LINK TO CREATION PLANS
People "I will make you into a great nation" (verse 2).	This will be developed in God's covenant with Abraham's descendants: "I will be your God and you will be my people" (Leviticus 26:12).	Fulfilment of command to Adam and Eve to "be fruitful and multiply". The promised "serpent-crusher" of Genesis 3:15 will come from Abraham's family.
Land "To your offspring I will give this land" (verse 7).	Abraham is told to move from his father's country and go to the land God shows him. This land is Canaan, the "Promised Land".	Adam and Eve had been cast out of Eden – the place of relationship with God. The Promised Land will be a sort of new Eden.
Blessing "I will bless you... all peoples on earth will be blessed through you" (verses 2, 3).	Blessing to Abraham and his family. But through Abraham's offspring blessing will go to the whole world. From the outset, God's people had a mission of bringing blessing to the world.	The fall brought curse. God's gospel promise to Abraham will bring blessing. The chief blessing is relationship with God himself – what humanity was originally made for.

LOOKING AHEAD TO JESUS:
The offspring of Abraham

These are the promises Jesus came to fulfil. These are the promises that the apostle Paul calls the "gospel" (Galatians 3:8). Jesus is the offspring of Abraham, in whom all peoples on earth will be blessed. Of course, the people in Abraham's day didn't know all this yet. There will be many partial fulfilments of these promises before Jesus arrives on the scene. But as God made these promises to Abraham, as he began the great drama of rescue and redemption, his plan was always that these promises would be fulfilled in Jesus Christ. Jesus will have a people from all nations, he will bring them to the glorious land of the new creation, and there they will enjoy God's blessing forever.

Opposition

God has a plan of blessing the world through the offspring of Abraham. But from the outset there will be opposition: some people will curse Abraham and his offspring, but they themselves will be judged (verse 3). This is a continuation of the conflict promised in Genesis 3:15. God's people should expect opposition, but ultimately vindication. Blessing will be offered to all peoples – but it will only be received by those who align themselves with Abraham and his offspring. Ultimately it will be a person's response to Jesus – the true "offspring of Abraham" – that will determine whether someone receives the blessings of Abraham or not.

COVENANT WITH ABRAHAM: "I WILL BE YOUR GOD"

Abraham received extraordinary promises from God. Yet there was more to come. God made a *covenant* with Abraham, showing he wanted *relationship* with his people. The chief promise of the covenant was "I will be their God" (Genesis 17:8) – a refrain which echoes through all the Scriptures. The story of the Bible is not of humanity seeking God, but of God seeking humanity, and pursuing relationship with them.

Abraham's descendants would be as numerous as the stars

Abraham's faith

The Lord appeared to Abraham again, to confirm and expand on the promises he had given him in Genesis 12. Despite Abraham being childless, God promised him that his descendants would be as numerous as the stars in the sky.

Abraham's response is vital: "Abram believed the LORD, and he credited it to him as righteousness" (Genesis 15:6). This is the first mention of faith (which means "belief" or "trust") in the Bible. Despite his wife Sarah's barrenness, Abraham believed that God had the power to do what he promised. In this way he is the model of faith. The apostle Paul calls him "the man of faith" (Galatians 3:9).

Abraham believed God, and God counted it as righteousness. God considered Abraham righteous (which means acceptable in God's sight) on the basis of his faith, not on the basis of any good things Abraham did. It is from Abraham that Paul gets his doctrine of justification by faith (Romans 4:1–3, see p. 142).

Abraham's obedience

God gave Abraham responsibilities as part of this covenant. He and every male in his family were to be circumcised, as a sign of the covenant, and Abraham duly obeyed. Abraham's obedience is most clearly seen years later when a son had been born to him in his old age: Isaac. The Lord told Abraham to take his son Isaac up a mountain and sacrifice him there. Isaac was the long-awaited child, beloved by his parents and the one through whom God's promises were to be fulfilled. Yet Abraham was prepared to obey God, believing that God had power to keep his promises – even to raise Isaac from the dead (Hebrews 11:19). At the last minute, God spoke to Abraham and told him to stay his hand. The Lord provided a ram caught in nearby bushes to be the sacrifice instead, and Isaac was freed (Genesis 22:13).

An angel prevents Abraham from sacrificing Isaac, from a book of Old Testament Stories, c.1880

Going deeper: Justified by faith or by works?

It seems there is a tension. Paul builds much on the fact that Abraham was justified by *faith*, but the epistle of James seems to give a different message: "Was not our father Abraham considered righteous for what he *did* when he offered his son Isaac on the altar?" (James 2:21, emphasis added). Even in Genesis, the Lord could say that he would keep his promises "*because* Abraham obeyed me and did everything I required of him, keeping my commands, my decrees and my instructions" (Genesis 26:5, emphasis added). The relationship between faith and good works is one of the most tricky and important doctrines in the Bible.

Paul and James are not contradicting each other, they are merely answering different questions. Paul is answering the question about the basis on which God counts people as righteous. Paul appeals to the example of Abraham to prove that it is not on the basis of anything he did, but merely his faith. After all, Abraham was counted righteous many years before he took his son Isaac to be sacrificed.

James is answering the question about what faith looks like. He appeals to Abraham to show that faith is not merely giving lip-service to some truths. Faith is real trust in God, which will inevitably lead to obedience and good works. Abraham being willing to sacrifice his son Isaac is the sure demonstration that his faith is real, not merely a show.

The covenant of grace

God's grace – his unmerited favour – is the dominant emphasis in this covenant. Abraham had done nothing to deserve the amazing blessings he was promised. Nor were the blessings conditional on his perfect obedience – as Adam and Eve's blessings had been. This marks a change in the way God related to his people. God's covenant with Adam could be described as a covenant of works – requiring perfect obedience. But after the fall in Genesis 3, such a covenant would never lead to blessing, as human sin was so inevitable. God's covenant with Abraham was a covenant of *grace* because the blessings would come through God's generosity, and would not have to be earned in any way.

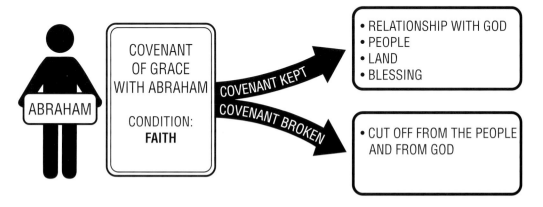

ABRAHAM

COVENANT OF GRACE WITH ABRAHAM

CONDITION: **FAITH**

COVENANT KEPT

COVENANT BROKEN

- RELATIONSHIP WITH GOD
- PEOPLE
- LAND
- BLESSING

- CUT OFF FROM THE PEOPLE AND FROM GOD

LOOKING AHEAD TO JESUS:
The true sacrifice

The story of the sacrifice of Isaac is a shocking one to modern readers. The picture of a father prepared to sacrifice his own son rightly raises emotions. The location is significant: Moriah, which is where Jerusalem would one day be built. When Isaac walked up that hill with wood on his back, he was doing what Jesus would do, centuries later. Even though the Lord stayed Abraham's hand, Isaac still underwent a sort of death and resurrection. In his case, the Lord provided a ram to be sacrificed instead.

Jesus is the true and greater Isaac, willingly put to death by his father so that blessing could come to the world. He is also is the true and greater ram, sacrificed in the place of his people. This is a shocking story because it speaks of a God who is willing to do violence to himself so that his people might enjoy blessing and life.

Jesus gives the illustration of a tree. Just as fruit is the sign that the tree is living, so obedience is a sign that a believer's faith is a living faith (John 15:1–8)

ISAAC, JACOB, AND JOSEPH: RELENTLESS GRACE

God had given Abraham astonishing promises: a land, a people, and blessing for all nations. God would fulfil his original creation purposes through Abraham and his offspring. Yet Abraham's family is utterly dysfunctional. They are not flawless heroes, but bitter, selfish, and immoral. The only hero in these chapters is God himself, who calls light out of darkness and uses weak people to carry his glorious promises forward.

"This is the account of…"

The book of Genesis is structured by a repeated heading "this is the account of" (NIV), each time introducing a new family line. This repeated formula highlights the search for the "offspring of the woman" from Genesis 3:15, the line of blessing. Not all of Abraham's children belong to the line of blessing, and the same is true for his son Isaac's children. Tim Chester has the following diagram to help us identify this line of blessing.

Isaac

Abraham had two sons, but the line of promise passes through Isaac, not Ishmael. Isaac was the child of promise, a miraculous birth, whereas Ishmael had been born when Abraham tried to "help God out" by sleeping with his maidservant and getting a son that way. The promises will be realized through God's miraculous intervention, not human effort.

God gave Isaac the same promises he gave Abraham: people, land, and blessing (Genesis 26:3–4). Isaac married Rebekah, which was important because she was from Abraham's people. If the line of blessing was to pass through Isaac and his family, his wife needed to be a worshipper of the Lord, not of foreign gods.

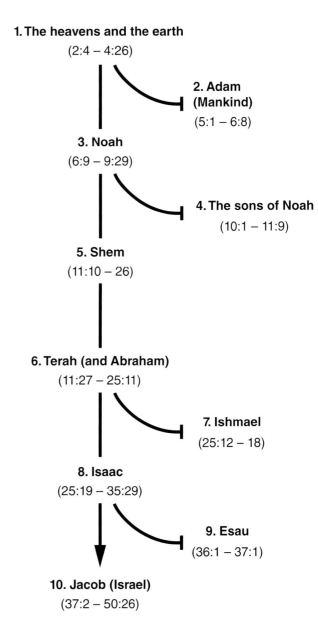

1. **The heavens and the earth**
(2:4 – 4:26)

2. **Adam (Mankind)**
(5:1 – 6:8)

3. **Noah**
(6:9 – 9:29)

4. **The sons of Noah**
(10:1 – 11:9)

5. **Shem**
(11:10 – 26)

6. **Terah (and Abraham)**
(11:27 – 25:11)

7. **Ishmael**
(25:12 – 18)

8. **Isaac**
(25:19 – 35:29)

9. **Esau**
(36:1 – 37:1)

10. **Jacob (Israel)**
(37:2 – 50:26)

Jacob

Isaac and Rebekah had two sons, who were twins. It was expected that the line of promise would pass through Esau, the oldest. But the Lord intervened and named Jacob as the chosen one. The apostle Paul highlights that God's choice of Jacob was not because he was more moral: God chose him "before the twins were born or had done anything good or bad – in order that God's purpose in election might stand" (Romans 9:11). Esau sold his birthright to his younger brother for a bowl of stew when he was hungry. But Jacob – whose name means deceiver – was no better. He deceived his dying father by dressing up as his brother to receive his father's blessing. He was no virtuous hero. Yet he received the same promises as Abraham and Isaac before him (Genesis 28:13–15).

The Lord watched over Jacob. Despite being driven from his homeland when Esau wanted to kill him, despite being tricked by his uncle Laban into marrying the wrong girl, despite being small in number and vulnerable, his family was protected. The Lord changed his name to Israel, and he fathered twelve sons, who would go on to form the twelve tribes of Israel.

Joseph

The last chapters of Genesis focus on Jacob's son Joseph. Here the narrative slows down again, taking thirteen chapters to cover Joseph's life. God disappears almost completely from the narrative. The narrator skilfully describes events from the point of view of the characters themselves, who can't see where God is or what he is doing.

Joseph was the favoured brother among the twelve sons of Jacob, and he had dreams that his brothers would one day bow down to him. Unsurprisingly, this made the other brothers jealous,

The burial of Jacob, from the fifteenth-century Nuremberg Bible

so one day in the country they planned to kill him, but then sold him instead into slavery (Genesis 37). Joseph was taken to Egypt, and sold to Potiphar, one of Pharaoh's officers. He served faithfully there, until Potiphar's wife tried to seduce him, then accused him of assaulting her. So he was thrown in prison, where he languished for years. The promises of God seemed to be languishing also.

Joseph dreams of the Sun, Moon, eleven stars and sheaves of wheat bowing down to him

Judah

At the end of Genesis we feel certain that Joseph must be one through whom promises will be fulfilled, but in a final twist, as Jacob blesses his sons, it is Judah who receives the promise of kingship (Genesis 49:10).

Judah was no saint. His sons had been put to death for wickedness. He sold his brother to slave traders. He slept with his daughter-in-law thinking she was a prostitute. Yet this is the man God will use to further his purposes.

God's people are not spiritual heroes. They are not those who have earned anything through their good deeds. Rather they are people who are – to borrow the title of a book by Iain Duguid – "Living in the grip of relentless grace".

LOOKING AHEAD TO JESUS:
God was working for good

In the story of Joseph, God was working behind the scenes. God enabled Joseph to interpret dreams, and this led him to interpreting dreams for the Pharaoh, being appointed prime minister, and saving Egypt from a famine. Joseph's brothers came to Egypt to buy grain because of the famine, and they ended up bowing down to Joseph just as Joseph had dreamed so many years before.

Joseph explained to his brothers how even their sinful actions – and indeed every other detail in the story – was part of God's good plan: "You intended to harm me, but God intended it for good to accomplish what is now being done, the saving of many lives" (Genesis 50:20). The story of Joseph foreshadows that of Jesus. Jesus was betrayed and put to death by wicked men, but this was all part of God's sovereign plan, to achieve the saving of many lives (Acts 2:23).

SLAVES IN EGYPT: MOSES AND PHARAOH

As the book of Exodus opens, in the shadow of the pyramids, Jacob's refugee family have become a great nation. God's hand has been upon them, and they have become "fruitful" and "multiplied greatly". The language echoes God's command to Adam and Eve – "be fruitful and multiply" – as well as God's promise to Abraham: "I will make you a great nation". Despite the famine in Canaan, despite the scheming of Jacob's sons, God's good plans are coming to pass. All seems well, until a new pharaoh, who does not know of Joseph, comes to power...

"More bricks!" (Exodus 1)

The new pharaoh saw that the Israelites had become numerous, and he was afraid. So he enslaved the Israelites and set taskmasters over them (Exodus 1:11). Sweltering under the relentless Egyptian sun, the Israelites were forced to build store cities for Pharaoh. Yet the Israelites continued to prosper, and so Pharaoh treated them more and more harshly. "More bricks" was Pharaoh's refrain, constantly demanding more and more from the Israelites, eventually even refusing to provide them the straw with which to make the bricks, yet still requiring the same number to be made.

Pharaoh is an "offspring of the serpent" figure (see p. 20), and the rest of the Bible sees Pharaoh as a picture of Satan himself. Rescue from his harsh rule is one of the dominant images the New Testament uses to picture salvation: "[God has] rescued us from the dominion of darkness and brought us into the kingdom of the Son he loves" (Colossians 1:13).

The Pyramids at Giza, Egypt

Moses was hidden in a basket and put into the River Nile.

A tale of two kingdoms

In Exodus 1–2, Pharaoh and the Lord are deliberately contrasted, so that later generations of Israelites and indeed Christians today could decide where their loyalties lie. Which "god" do they want to follow? Which kingdom do they want to live in?

PHARAOH/SATAN	GOD
Desires to restrict: "the Israelites have become much too numerous for us" (Exodus 1:9).	Desires blessing and growth: "Be fruitful and multiply" (Genesis 1:28, ESV).
Oppressive and abusive. Uses the Israelites for his own ends. Constantly demands more.	Hears the cries of his people, and is concerned about their suffering. Liberates his people.
God of death: gives a command that all the Hebrew boys must be killed (Exodus 1:16).	God of life: gives children to the faithful Hebrew midwives who refuse to kill the babies (Exodus 1:21). (The midwives were most likely women unable to have children.)
Ultimately powerless. He fails to prevent the Israelites from becoming "even more numerous".	Powerful and sovereign. His plans succeed and he is seen to be the true God.

The birth of Moses

God heard the cries of his people and was concerned about their suffering, so he raised up a deliverer, Moses. The account of Moses' birth is full of allusions to previous stories in the Bible. When Moses was born, his mother saw that "he was good" (an echo of the creation account "it was good") and so hid him for three months. Moses was placed in a basket (the same word as for Noah's "ark") in the Nile, and was saved from death through water, just as Noah was (Exodus 2:1–10). Like Noah, Moses is a "new creation" figure.

Baby Moses in the basket was found by Pharaoh's daughter, so not only did Moses escape death, he grew up with all the privileges of an Egyptian, more than that, of a royal child. Yet Moses refused to enjoy these privileges whilst he saw his own people suffering: " [Moses] chose to be mistreated along with the people of God rather than to enjoy the fleeting pleasures of sin" (Hebrews 11:25). Moses saw beyond his present circumstances to the future fulfilment of the promises of God – and as such he is one of the great Old Testament examples of *faith*.

The burning bush

Despite this faith, Moses was still far from being ready to rescue his people. One day, after he had grown up, he saw one of his own people being beaten by an Egyptian, so he killed the Egyptian. When this was discovered, he was forced to flee to live to the desert. There in the desert God appeared to him, at a bush that was burning with fire, yet was not consumed (Exodus 3). God told Moses that he had heard the cries of the Israelites, and so was sending Moses to bring them out of Egypt.

From the burning bush, God revealed his "name" to Moses. In the Hebrew world, names were very important as they revealed something of the person's character. God revealed his name as "Yahweh" (often rendered LORD in English translations), which in Hebrew sounds like "I am" or "I am who I am". This name speaks of God's freedom and sovereignty, and in a later passage beginning and ending with "I am Yahweh" God reveals more of what this name means:

- He is the *saviour*: "I will bring you out from under the yoke of the Egyptians. I will free you from being slaves to them, and I will redeem you with an outstretched arm and with mighty acts of judgment" (Exodus 6:6).
- He wants *relationship* with his people: "I will take you as my own people, and I will be your God" (Exodus 6:7).
- He keeps his *covenant promises*: "I will bring you to the land I swore with uplifted hand to give to Abraham, to Isaac and to Jacob" (Exodus 6:8).

LOOKING AHEAD TO JESUS: "I am"

Jesus deliberately picked up on God's Old Testament name of "I am" when debating with the Jewish leaders. When they questioned his authority, Jesus responded not simply that he was greater than their hero Abraham, but that "before Abraham was born, I am!" (John 8:58). By calling himself "I am" – which he would do seven more times in John's Gospel – Jesus was clearly identifying himself as the God of the Old Testament who had revealed himself to Moses. Jesus was God come to earth as saviour, wanting relationship, and keeping all God's promises.

THE EXODUS: GOD REDEEMED HIS PEOPLE

God's people were in distress. Yet Pharaoh would not want to lose this nation of slaves, and his army was the most powerful in the known world. How could God's people escape? It looks impossible. With the Lord's repeated command to Pharaoh "let my people go!" and the ten plagues, this is one of the most dramatic stories in the Bible. Pharaoh's question "Who is the Lord?" drives the whole narrative. As God rescues his people from cruel slavery, he will demonstrate the strength of his arm and the tenderness of his heart.

Plagues

The ten plagues on Egypt are perhaps the most well-known passages in Exodus (chapters 7–11). Through Moses, the Lord tells Pharaoh to let his people go, and threatens plagues if he refuses. On some occasions, Pharaoh does say he will let the people go, but then each time he hardens his heart, and does not keep his promise.

1. The Nile turns to blood.	6. Boils break out on all the Egyptians.
2. Frogs cover the land of Egypt.	7. Hail falls, killing crops and animals.
3. Gnats rise up from the dust.	8. Locusts swarm over the land, devouring crops.
4. Flies fill the land.	9. Darkness covers the whole land for three days.
5. Egyptian livestock die.	10. Death of the firstborn.

Painting of the Egyptian god Ra and Maat from the tomb of Tausert and Setnakht in the Valley of the Kings, Luxor

Why ten plagues?

Why didn't God win the victory over Pharaoh instantly? Why ten plagues? The answer comes in an oft-repeated phrase in these chapters of Exodus: "By this you will know that I am the Lord" (Exodus 7:17). God orchestrated these events to demonstrate his power and majesty. The universe is not in a power struggle between good and evil. God is utterly in control, even over a powerful and evil figure like Pharaoh. Pharaoh is responsible for his actions, but God is also sovereign and uses this confrontation with Pharaoh to display his glory in the earth:

> Then the Lord said to Moses, "Go to Pharaoh, for I have hardened his heart and the hearts of his officials **so that** I may do these miraculous signs of mine among them, and **so that** you may tell your son and grandson how severely I dealt with the Egyptians and performed miraculous signs among them, and you will know that I am the Lord."
>
> Exodus 10:1–2, CSB, emphasis added

The Passover: Salvation through judgment

The final plague was the death of all the firstborn: a fitting judgment on Pharaoh who had himself oppressed Israel, God's "son", and had even tried to kill all the firstborn boys. This final plague would be a just judgment for sin; but the Israelites too were sinful, and so the Lord needed to provide a way for them to be saved through the judgment. Each family was to kill a lamb and daub the blood over the door, so that when the Lord went through the land to strike down the Egyptians, he would "pass over" that house where he saw the blood (Exodus 12:12–13). And so it happened as the Lord had said. There was not a house that night where there was not a death – either the firstborn son, or the lamb in the son's place.

God commanded the people to remember this night and celebrate this "Passover" celebration every year. Fundamental to their identity was that they had been *redeemed*. A price had been paid – the death of a lamb – to secure their freedom. This was to be the subject of their songs and stories, and in future times of distress, the people could look back to the Exodus and remember that God was a God who *saved*.

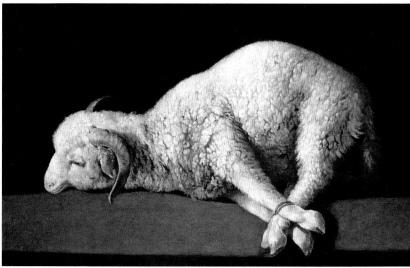

Agnus Dei (Lamb of God) by Francisco Zurbaran

Crossing the Red Sea: Salvation by judgment

After the plague on the firstborn, the Lord led the people out of Egypt, but they were pursued by the Egyptian army. They ended up trapped, with the army on one side, and the Red Sea (or perhaps the Reed Sea) on the

Exodus by Richard Mcbee, showing the parting of the Red Sea

other. The Lord told Moses to stretch out his staff over the sea, and the Lord drove the sea back, making a way for the Israelites to pass through on dry land. Then, when the Egyptians pursued them, the Lord caused the sea to come back upon the Egyptians and drown their whole army (Exodus 14:28). As with the plagues, this happened so the Israelites and the Egyptians would "know that I am the LORD" (Exodus 14:18).

The Lord redeemed his people, but he did so by crushing the oppressor. Salvation for God's people can only be achieved if evil is judged and defeated forever.

LOOKING AHEAD TO JESUS:
The Passover lamb

Centuries after the exodus, Jesus sat with his disciples in an upper room, eating the Passover meal. But rather than speaking of exodus from Egypt and the Passover lamb, he spoke of his impending death. Jesus was the greater Passover lamb, the one who would die in the place of his people and free them from slavery. Just as the firstborn Israelites were to look to the lamb that had died in their place for their assurance, so too with Christians. Christians are not to look to their own morality to save them through the coming judgment. Rather they are to look to the blood of the Passover lamb – Jesus Christ – killed in their place.

MOUNT SINAI: THE LAW AND THE COVENANT

The mountain burns with smoke and fire. A lone trumpet blast pierces the darkness and thick smoke. The ground quakes, the sky is torn apart, and creation itself groans under the weight of the glory of the Lord as he descends upon Sinai. God tells the people not to approach the mountain lest they die, but such instruction barely seems necessary, as they tremble in fear before the awesome presence of God...

The covenant with Moses at Sinai

After leading his people through the Red Sea, God brought them to meet with him in the desert at Mount Sinai (Exodus 19), where he gave them his laws. It is scarcely possible to overestimate the drama of the scene. It shows the utter power, majesty, and holiness of God, which makes the gracious words he speaks all the more amazing. God makes a covenant with his people. He says he wants *relationship* with them. The covenant here is a reiteration and expansion of that made with Abraham. The key aspect added is that God will dwell amongst his people in the tabernacle.

Mount Sinai

The laws: Love for God, love for neighbour

The people remained at the foot of the mountain, whilst Moses ascended to the summit, where God gave him the laws. The laws begin with the foundational "Ten Commandments" (Exodus 20), written by God himself on two tablets of stone (Exodus 34).

1. You shall have no other gods before me.	6. You shall not murder.
2. You shall not make for yourself an idol.	7. You shall not commit adultery.
3. You shall not misuse the name of the Lord your God.	8. You shall not steal.
4. Remember the Sabbath day by keeping it holy.	9. You shall not give false testimony.
5. Honour your father and your mother.	10. You shall not covet.

The Ten Commandments on the wall near King David's Tomb in Jerusalem

These are followed by other laws: the outworking of the Ten Commandments in particular situations. Though there are many laws, they may be summed up as "Love God" and "Love your neighbour" (Matthew 22:35–40).

Love God. God demands unique devotion and affection from his people because of who he is and what he has done.

Love your neighbour. Running through all the laws is a focus on the sanctity of human life, and care for the vulnerable such as the poor, the widow, and the foreigner. Right from the start, care for those who are different was a vital part of what it meant to be God's people, because this reflects the heart of God himself.

This covenant is not about earning salvation. These laws are given to a people who have *already* been redeemed. Even the Ten Commandments themselves begin with a reminder of what God has first done: "I am the Lord your God, who brought you out of Egypt, out of the land of slavery" (Exodus 20:2). For the people in the Old Testament, just as in the New, salvation is not based on any good that people do. God first saves people, *then* calls them to holy living as a response to what he has already done.

Going deeper: Conditional or unconditional?

Some see a tension between the covenant with Abraham and the covenant with Moses. They see the covenant with Abraham as being unconditional, whereas the covenant with Moses depends on perfect obedience.

The covenant with Moses *does* emphasize obedience: "*if* you obey me fully and keep my covenant, then out of all nations you will be my treasured possession" (Exodus 19:5). But it is still a *gracious* covenant. God gave the sacrificial system to make forgiveness available. The heart of both the covenants with Abraham and Moses is *faith*. The focus in the covenant with Moses is on how this faith should be expressed in sincere – even though not perfect – obedience.

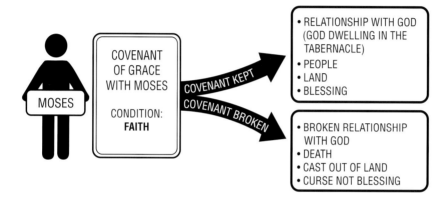

LOOKING AHEAD TO JESUS: *Justice and mercy*

The LORD, the LORD, the compassionate and gracious, slow to anger, abounding in love and faithfulness, maintaining love to thousands, and forgiving wickedness, rebellion and sin. Yet he does not leave the guilty unpunished.

Exodus 34:6–7

When God proclaims his "name" he is revealing the heart of his character. But what he reveals about himself seems almost contradictory: he won't leave the wicked unpunished, but he will also forgive. How can these both be true of God?

These words spoken to Moses point ahead to Jesus and his death in the place of his people (see p. 128). This is where God's just judgment and his merciful forgiveness would be seen. In Jesus, God's character is most clearly revealed.

The golden calf

Tragically, while Moses was up the mountain receiving God's law, the people down below became impatient and made an idol – a golden calf. They wanted a god they could control and domesticate. They wanted a god that could be seen.

Even after all God has done for his people, their hearts still turn away from him. This would be the problem all through the Old Testament. The covenant with Moses was good, but the people's hearts kept turning away.

THE TABERNACLE: GOD DWELLS AMONG US

14

The great tragedy so far in the Bible story was when God's people were thrown down from their mountain sanctuary, the Garden of Eden. Would they be able to re-ascend into the presence of the Lord? Could they again dwell with God, or must they forever remain at a distance?

The goal of redemption: "I will dwell among them"

God met with his people at Mount Sinai in great glory and majesty as he gave them the law, but even this was not the final goal of redemption from slavery. The great goal of redemption is expressed in the central promise of Exodus: "Then have them make a sanctuary for me, and I will dwell among them" (Exodus 25:8).

According to the Bible, the purpose of human existence is to dwell with God: "One thing I ask from the LORD, this only do I seek; that I may dwell in the house of the LORD all the days of my life, to gaze on the beauty of the LORD and to seek him in his temple" (Psalm 27:4).

As one writer has put it: "Entering the house of God to dwell with God, beholding, glorifying and enjoying him eternally, I suggest, is *the* story of the Bible, the plot that makes sense of the various acts, persons and places of its pages, the deepest context for its doctrines."[7]

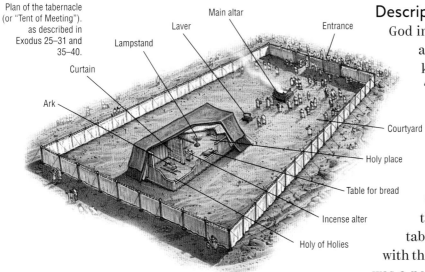

Plan of the tabernacle (or "Tent of Meeting"). as described in Exodus 25–31 and 35–40.

Main altar
Laver
Entrance
Lampstand
Curtain
Ark
Courtyard
Holy place
Table for bread
Incense alter
Holy of Holies

Description of the tabernacle

God instructed the people to build a richly ornamented tent known as the tabernacle or "tent of meeting". During the time in the wilderness, this would be where God dwelt amongst his people – a "royal tent" in the heart of the camp. Once the people reached the Promised Land, the tabernacle would be replaced with the Temple in Jerusalem, which was a permanent structure, but with the same overall layout.

The layout and the furniture all taught a theological message: of separation between God and his people, and the barriers needing to be crossed to enter: sacrifices and washing. The centre of the tabernacle was the Holy of Holies, God's throne room where heaven touched earth. This was where the Ark of the Covenant was kept, the box containing the stone tablets of the Ten Commandments. Only the high priest was allowed to enter here, and only once a year on the Day of Atonement (see p. 44).

Cherubim guarding the way

The tabernacle was an extraordinary privilege for Israel. Exodus ends with it being filled with the glory of the Lord – he had come to dwell amidst his people. But Moses was not able to enter. The people were not yet back in God's paradise presence: like Adam and Eve, they still had to stay at a distance because of their sin. The cherubim guarding the way to the Holy of Holies symbolized that the way back into God's presence was closed. Like Sinai, the tabernacle was a place of threat as well as blessing. Trying to enter God's presence without his express invitation would result in certain death, as Aaron's sons Nadab and Abihu later found out (Leviticus 10:1–2).

But God had still promised, "I will dwell among the Israelites and be their God" (Exodus 29:45). How can this be? How can sinful man dwell with a holy God? Who can ascend the hill of the Lord? These are the questions that will be addressed by the next book, Leviticus.

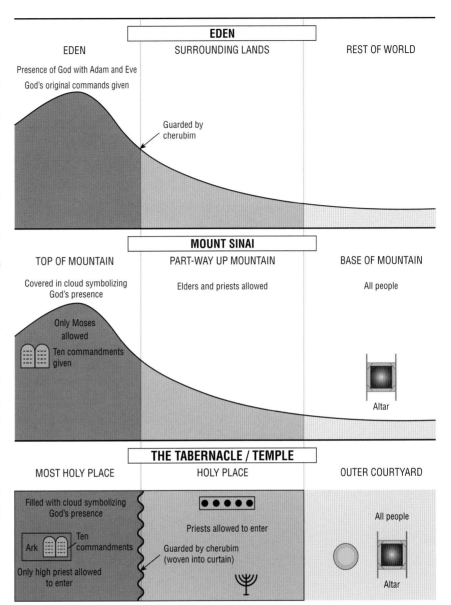

The correspondences between Eden, Sinai and the tabernacle/Temple

 LOOKING AHEAD TO JESUS:
Re-entering God's presence

When Jesus died on the cross, the Temple curtain was torn in two from top to bottom. Jesus' death was the ultimate means of humanity being allowed back in the presence of God, of returning to Eden.

LEVITICUS: HOLINESS, PRIESTS, AND SACRIFICE

Leviticus can feel alien to modern readers, with all the sacrificial deaths and the strange rituals and laws about cleanliness. In fact, however, it is a book about *life*. The sacrifices in the first half of the book all point to how life with God is possible. The holiness laws that make up the second half all point to how life with God can be enjoyed.

Fresco showing Aaron as High Priest from Altlerchenfelder church, Vienna

Sacrifice: Approaching a holy God

Leviticus is at the heart of the Pentateuch and answers its central question: how can a holy God dwell with a sinful people? The answer is through sacrifice and through what it achieves: "atonement". This word has two senses: cleansing from sin and appeasing God's wrath. The penalty for sin is death, but the sacrificial animal – usually a bull or goat or lamb – dies as a substitute so that the worshipper may be cleansed and live. This explains the emphasis on blood in the sacrifices: blood represents the life poured out and symbolizes the death that is the just punishment for sin (Leviticus 17:11).

The sacrifices were not primarily a gift to God (as if he needed anything) but were gifts from God to enable the people to continue in relationship with him. They were to be offered by the priests God had appointed and in the manner God directed. God's people could have confidence as they approached him but they were not to be casual or complacent. Underpinning the whole system was faith. The people were not merely to go through the motions but they were to trust in God's gracious provision of a substitute to pay for their sin.

The sacrifices

There are five main types of sacrifice in Leviticus. The order of the sacrifices in Leviticus 9 points to the astonishing fact that God's people were not merely cleansed and able to enter the presence of God but were also invited to dine with him.

CLEANSING		COMMITMENT		COMMUNION
Sin offering and/or guilt offering.		Burnt offering (with accompanying grain offering).		Fellowship/peace offering.
Key feature: sprinkling of blood.	→ Needed for:	Key feature: whole animal is burnt up.	→ Leads to:	Key feature: the people feast together, eating the sacrificed animal.
Signifies cleansing from sin.		Signifies total commitment of worshipper. Also appeases God's anger at sin.		Signifies fellowship (communion) with God.

Clean and unclean

Leviticus contains many laws about clean and uncleanness. Some make sense at the level of food hygiene but many do not, because, according to Leviticus, uncleanness is primarily about relationship with God. Uncleanness is a problem because it will defile God's tabernacle, resulting in death for the one who defiled it (Leviticus 15:31). Objects and people are classified into one of three states, which relate to how close one may approach to God.

Sin and death →

Holy (specially belonging to God).	Clean (fit for the presence of God).	Unclean (must be kept away from God).

← Sacrifice

The holiness laws of Leviticus may seem perplexing to modern readers. But they were a good gift from God, intended to prevent the people becoming unclean and cast out of his presence. But sin was inevitable, as was contact with death (which underpins some of the harder to understand laws). The only means of restoration was *sacrifice*.

A goat was killed as a sin offering

Day of Atonement: Leviticus 16

The centre of Leviticus, the centre of the whole Pentateuch, the centre of Israel's calendar and life, was the Day of Atonement. The climax of this ceremony is the high priest entering into the Holy of Holies. This is the closest humanity has entered into the presence of God since Adam and Eve in the Garden of Eden. Nadab and Abihu tried to enter on their own terms, but died. There is no safe way back into Eden other than the way God himself provides. This ceremony, which happened once every year, centres on two goats, both of which represent the people.

	WHAT HAPPENED	WHAT IT ACHIEVED
First goat – for purification	The first goat is taken into the tabernacle and killed as a sin offering.	The tabernacle and the people were cleansed from all their sins.
Second goat – scapegoat	Sins of the people are confessed over the second goat – symbolically laying sins on the goat. Goat is driven east out of the camp into the wilderness to die. It is cast out of the presence of God, into exile and death, just as Adam and Eve were and just as the people deserved.	Pictures sins being carried away, never to return. As a result of the goat being cast out, the high priest (as a representative of the people) is able to enter into the Holy of Holies and the presence of God himself, the exact reverse of what happened to Adam at the fall.

LOOKING AHEAD TO JESUS:
The full and final sacrifice

The sacrificial system repeatedly proclaimed to the people the whole story of the Bible in miniature: sin led to humanity becoming unclean and being cast from the presence of God. The only way back was through the means God provided: a pure and spotless blood sacrifice dying in one's place. God gave this centuries-long visual aid so his people would understand the meaning of Jesus' death. Jesus was the full and final sacrifice to which the whole sacrificial system pointed. This is why Christians no longer offer sacrifices – Jesus' death was sufficient to pay for the sins of all his people for all time. This includes Old Testament believers. Old Testament believers really experienced forgiveness through the sacrificial system, as they trusted God's provision of a substitute. But it was only when Christ died that the penalty for their sins was actually paid for.

NUMBERS: WILDERNESS WANDERINGS

The book of Numbers picks up the narrative where Exodus left off. After an extended period at Mount Sinai receiving the laws, the people have set out towards the Promised Land of Canaan. It is only an eleven-day journey, and the Lord is in their midst. The blessings of God – in particular the blessing of land – seem on the near horizon. Yet not eleven days later, but *forty years* later the people stand on the brink of the Promised Land, with a whole generation having died out in the desert. What went wrong?

Arrangement of the camp of Israel Numbers 2:1 – 3:39

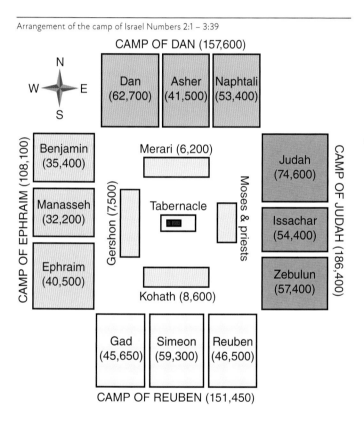

Arrangement of the camp

The book of Numbers begins in an upbeat fashion. The people were now a great multitude: 603,550 (Numbers 1:46). God gave them instructions of how to arrange the camp on the journey, with his royal tent at the centre. God was truly in the midst of his people – the words "tabernacle" and "tent of meeting" are used thirty-two and fifty-four times respectively. Yet the priests were to camp between the tabernacle and the other tribes, ensuring that no one transgressed on the Lord's holiness. Similarly, the Lord prescribed in great detail how the tabernacle and the Ark of the Covenant were to be moved. God's presence is a blessing, but also a threat. A pillar of cloud covered the tabernacle as a sign of God's presence; when the people were to move, the cloud moved and led the people.

Manna in the desert

Though they were in the wilderness, the Lord provided them food – "manna", a bread from heaven. This appeared each day with the morning dew, enough for everyone to have just what they needed. If anyone tried to keep some until the next day, it bred maggots and stank. The only exception was the sabbath day, when no manna appeared. On the day before the sabbath the people were to collect twice as much, and this didn't get maggots when it was kept overnight (Exodus 16:1–35).

As well as being a miraculous provision, this was also intended to teach the people about God. Every morning they woke up with no food. Every day they had to depend on the Lord. And every day for forty years they had enough. Jesus intended his disciples to think of this incident when he taught them to pray, "Give us today our daily bread" (Matthew 6:11).

The people also miraculously received water from a rock – once at the beginning of their journey (Exodus 17), once at the end (Numbers 20).

Distrust and disobedience

Despite their daily provision from the Lord, the people in Numbers complained repeatedly. They complained about the food the Lord provided (Numbers 11). Miriam and Aaron opposed Moses, jealous that he was the leader (Numbers 12). Worst of all, the people rejected the Promised Land itself. Before entering the land, some of the people were sent into the land as spies to see what it was like. They reported that the people there were strong and the cities well-fortified.

The people had a choice: would they trust in God to bring them into the land or not? Only Joshua and Caleb trusted God. Everyone else refused to enter the land, saying they had been better off in Egypt. As a result, the Lord promised that none of those who disobeyed would enter the Promised Land, but that they would die in the wilderness. This is what happened. For forty years the people wandered in the desert, until all the disobedient generation died out.

The apostle Paul reflects on these wilderness years and urges his readers not to make the same mistake of unbelief. The heart of the Christian life is *faith* – trusting God on the journey, trusting that he will provide, trusting that though the wilderness at times seems bleak, God will bring his people to their final home.

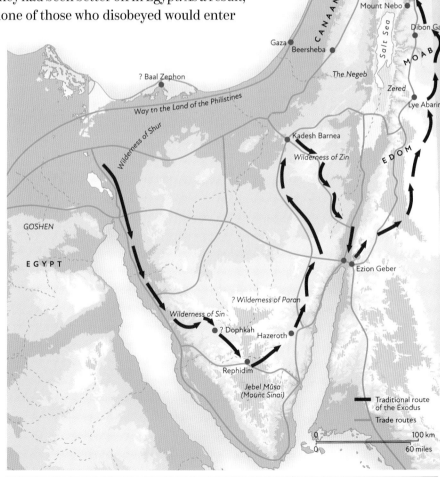

The people's journey from Egypt to the Promised Land

The desert wilderness of the Sinai peninsula

LOOKING AHEAD TO JESUS:

God's sustaining presence

The people in Numbers were strengthened for the journey by bread from heaven and water from a rock. Paul says it was ultimately Christ who was with them, providing all they needed (1 Corinthians 10:4). Christian believers know in a far deeper way the presence of Christ with them on their journey, by the life-giving waters of his spirit. "Even though I walk through the darkest valley, I will fear no evil, because Christ is with me" (adapted from Psalm 23).

Feasts

Yet even in this desert, winds of hope still blow. The Lord gave commands about the different feasts the people were to celebrate once in the land. This pointed to the certainty of entering the land, but also the joy and life that would be found there.

Passover	Celebrating deliverance from Egypt. The year began with the people remembering God's great act of rescue.
The Feast of Weeks (Pentecost)	A celebration of the firstfruits of the harvest, held seven weeks after Passover.
The Day of Atonement	The annual reminder of the need for forgiveness (see p. 44).
The Feast of Booths/ Tabernacles	For this festival the people lived in tents, to remind them of their wanderings in the wilderness.

17

DEUTERONOMY: "CHOOSE LIFE!"

Deuteronomy is a book for people on the threshold. God's people are camped in the plains of Moab, with just the River Jordan between them and the land of Canaan. This is the land promised to Abraham centuries before. They can almost smell the fragrance of the orchards and olive groves. Their wanderings are over; life in the Eden-like land is just about to begin. And so, with his final words before he dies, Moses urges the people to "choose life!" (Deuteronomy 30:19). These words were not just for the people of Moses' day. Deuteronomy was to be read every seven years in the land, a loud trumpet call ringing through the years calling the people to faithful obedience "today".

Love as the fulfilment of the law

Deuteronomy consists of three sermons given by Moses, re-presenting the law for the new generation. Deuteronomy highlights *love* in a way that has not been seen before: "Hear, O Israel: The LORD our God, the LORD is one. Love the LORD your God with all your heart and with all your soul and with all your strength" (Deuteronomy 6:4–5).

Though some of the details of the Commandments may seem strange to us today, they should be understood as answers to the questions "How can I love God?" and "How can I love my neighbour?" Love is also the motivation for keeping these commands. God's people don't obey him to try to earn favour, or out of a sense of grim duty. Rather they obey because they love the God who saved them.

It is vital to understand this. If the law is misused to try to earn favour from God, it becomes a crushing burden. Rightly understood, these laws were given "for your own good" (Deuteronomy 10:13). The laws were a good gift to the people, and part of how they would be a light to the nations (Deuteronomy 4:6–8).

View from Mount Nebo, where Moses first looked across into the Promised Land

Going deeper: The laws today

How do Christians view these Old Testament laws today? They show how far everyone has fallen from God's standard, and the need for forgiveness only available through Jesus Christ (Romans 3:19). But what about "keeping" the laws? Are these laws to teach Christians how to live? Or have they been superseded by the New Testament? There are two main views on this question:

"Lutheran" view	The laws of the Old Testament are not binding on Christians. Only from the commands of Christ do Christians learn how to live.	Strong discontinuity between OT and NT. Law is seen in opposition to gospel.
"Reformed" view	The law reveals people's sin, but also teaches Christian believers how to live – interpreted in the light of the coming of Christ.	More continuity between OT and NT. Law (if rightly used) is not in opposition to gospel.

Deuteronomy 6 (including the Shema) in Hebrew

שמע ישראל יהוה אלהינו יהוה אחד

The threefold division of the law

Traditionally, the Old Testament laws have been distinguished into three categories. While not perfect, this distinction helps summarize which laws continue for Christians today, and how.

Moral laws God's enduring standards – particularly the Ten Commandments	God's character remains the same in the Old and New Testament, and laws such as "do not murder", "do not commit adultery", "do not lie" are enduring moral commands for all time.
Ceremonial laws Laws relating to sacrifices and priests	The Old Testament sacrificial system ended when Christ died as the full and final sacrifice for sin. These laws no longer apply. Christians "keep" these laws today by trusting Christ's final sacrifice for sin at the cross.
Civil laws The government of the Israelite people in their land	Christians are not a nation–state, like Old Testament Israel, so these laws do not apply today. Yet there are timeless principles behind these laws that do continue – for example, justice, love of neighbour.

Entering the land

As the people enter the land, they are to remember that they are not being given the land because of their great numbers, because of their military prowess, or because of their righteousness (7:7; 8:17; 9:4). The land is being given to them as a *gift*, by God's grace. Yet they are not to be presumptuous. They are to remember God's covenant, and the requirement of obedient faith. No one is to think, "I will be safe, even though I persist in going my own way" (29:19). The book of Deuteronomy draws to an end with a list of blessings and curses: blessings if the people obey; curses if they disobey. Moses sets before the people "life and death, blessings and curses" and he urges them to "choose life" by responding to the Lord with obedient faith (30:19). Sadly, as the book closes, Moses promises that the people won't choose life, but will disobey and be cast out of the land. Even before they enter the land, the shadow of exile is looming over them.

LOOKING AHEAD TO JESUS:
Dealing with human sin

Deuteronomy begins and ends with failure. It starts by recounting the disobedience of the wilderness generation and finishes with the exile in view. More than any other, this book should drive God's people to their knees. If it were dependent on their own righteousness, God's blessings would be as elusive as trying to catch a rainbow. But Deuteronomy is full of hope. The blessings on offer are not built on the shifting sands of human merit, but on the bedrock of the promises of God.

Jesus is the one who deals with the sin that Deuteronomy so clearly reveals. Jesus is the one whose perfect obedience guarantees the blessings Deuteronomy promises. He is the one whose grace would transform his people's hearts, so that they could begin to love and serve God as Deuteronomy calls them to do.

JOSHUA: ENTERING THE PROMISED LAND

It was the end of an era. Moses, the towering figure who had dominated the story until now, had died. Yet as well as being a time of uncertainty, it was a time of hope for the people of God. The promises given to Abraham were taking shape. They had become a great nation in Egypt. At Mount Sinai they had been told the way of blessing: living in faithful obedience to God's law, with his presence in their midst. Now the promise of "land" was about to be fulfilled; not just a fulfilment of the promise to Abraham, but even a return of sorts to Eden...

Joshua as a new Moses

Joshua is commissioned to lead God's people, and he is very much presented as a new Moses figure. Like Moses, he would lead the people miraculously through water. Like Moses, he had an encounter with God where he had to remove his sandals (Joshua 5:13–15; Exodus 3:1–6). Most importantly, Joshua is promised that the Lord would be with him. This is the source of confidence for the people: not so much that they have a new Moses, but that the God who was with Moses was still with them and with their new leader, Joshua. The hero of the book of Joshua is not Joshua, but God himself.

Entering the land

The crossing of the River Jordan and entry into the Promised Land beyond is described in ways meant to evoke the Exodus. The Lord parts the Jordan river and the people pass through on dry ground. The Ark of the Covenant goes first: the Lord leads the way just as he had led the way out of Egypt. The goal of entry into the land is the same as the goal of the Exodus: that the Lord

The River Jordan

might display his glory – both to his own people, and to the nations (Joshua 2:9–11; 3:10; 4:24). A pattern is being set up which will recur throughout Scripture: God saves his people through the waters of judgment, to the praise of his glory.

Jericho

The first major city that the people came to was Jericho – a fortified walled city that they would have to conquer in order to enter and take possession of the land. One can hardly imagine a worse military strategy than what the Lord commands the people: marching around the town for seven days, each day blowing trumpets and shouting. There is no hidden secret here. As a human strategy it is utter foolishness. Yet on the seventh day, God caused the walls to fall down and gave the city into the hands of his people. God worked through human weakness – as he so often does in Scripture – and simply called his people to trust him, even when his ways seemed very strange. The taking of Jericho is a visual aid to highlight the central message of chapters 6–12: that the land is a *gift* of God.

Rahab

Jericho was completely destroyed, as would be other towns listed in these chapters. Yet not everyone died. Before the conquest, spies had been sent into the land to scout it out. In Jericho they had been found out, but hid in the house of Rahab, a prostitute. Rahab hid the men on the roof, under stalks of flax, and told the soldiers searching for them that they had gone a different way. Rahab let the men down by a rope through the window, because her house was built into the city wall. Before the men left she asked them to spare her and her family when they conquered Jericho, and she was told to tie a scarlet cord in her window as a sign. So when Jericho was taken, Rahab and her family were spared, and joined the people of God (Joshua 2; 6:25).

Rahab – a foreign prostitute – becomes a member of God's people, and more than that, will feature in Jesus' family tree (Matthew 1:5).

The Promised Land, rich and abundant with crops

The land as new Eden

The Promised Land is described as new Eden. It is a place of abundance and prosperity, it is a place where God will dwell with his people, and it is a place where God will give *rest* (Joshua 1:13; 11:23; 21:44). This also explains the significance of having to drive out the nations of the land, which forms a significant part of the middle section of the book. People that repent – like Rahab – can come and be part of God's people. But those that oppose God's people, and prove themselves to be "offspring of the serpent", must be driven out of the land, just as Adam should have driven out the unclean serpent from the garden.

The division of the land

There are a few minor notes in the book. Not all the inhabitants of the land are driven out (13:13; 17:12). Yet overall, the picture is positive. God gives "rest on every side"; every promise he has made is fulfilled (21:43–45). The land lay "subdued" before the people, showing that the people are starting to fulfil the original creation plan of "filling and subduing the earth" (Joshua 18:1; Genesis 1:28). The long lists of which parts of the land are given to which tribe may seem dull to modern readers, but all the detail should not obscure the main point: the people were being given a permanent residence in the kingdom of God where he was present to bless his people.

LOOKING AHEAD TO JESUS:

Rest

Hebrews chapter 3 says that the "rest" the people enjoyed in the Promised Land was not the end. There was a greater rest still to come. Jesus is the true and greater Joshua – indeed the name "Jesus" is simply the Greek version of the Hebrew name Joshua. Jesus is the faithful leader who brings his people safely through the waters of death and gives them rest: not in the earthly Promised Land but in the greater rest of the new creation kingdom of God.

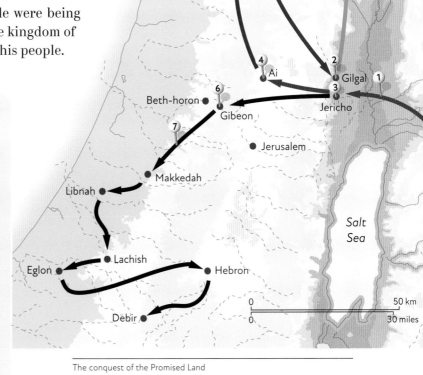

The conquest of the Promised Land

JUDGES: THE MISERY OF LIFE WITH NO KING

God has given Israel rest in their Promised Land, their new Eden. Like Adam and Eve, they have a blank canvas of opportunity, and a task of glorifying God throughout the earth. They are to be a holy nation, a royal priesthood. So much opportunity. So much hope. Yet the people thought life was better lived their own way. Judges begins the story of Israel's sin in their new Eden, which will ultimately lead to them being cast out to the East, just as Adam was.

Introduction: Military and spiritual decline after Joshua's death

After Joshua died, the people tried to complete the conquest of the land, but they failed to drive out all the nations – paralleling Adam's failure to cast the unclean serpent out of the garden. The people even tolerated the idols of the nations, and so God promised judgment on Israel, that these foreign nations would become "thorns" and snares to them, just as Adam and Eve's land was cursed with thorns and thistles (2:3).

The people served the Lord all the days of Joshua. But then "another generation grew up who neither knew the Lord nor what he had done for Israel" (2:10). The new generation didn't know the story of which they were part. Their parents hadn't obeyed the command of Deuteronomy to speak of the deeds of the Lord at all times (Deuteronomy 6:6–9; 20–24). As a result, the new generation "did evil in the eyes of the Lord" and "followed and worshipped various gods of the peoples round them" (Judges 2:11–12).

The days of the judges were dark times in Israel

The Judges

The main section of the book has a repeating cycle, beginning with the people's sin:

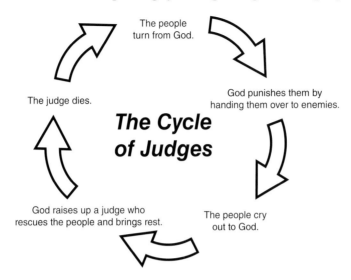

A period of nearly 1,000 years is covered here, from roughly 1200–1000 BC. There was no centralized government, but God raised up these occasional judges. They were chosen by God, and empowered by God's spirit. They acted as rulers, both settling disputes within God's people, but also delivering them from their enemies. They were men and women of faith, but were hardly models of godliness. Gideon obeyed the Lord by pulling down the altar of Baal, but he did it at night, as he was afraid (6:27). Jephthah killed his own daughter after making a rash vow (11:29–40).

Samson

The story of the final judge, Samson, reflects that of the nation. He was a Nazarite – set apart to be holy to God, just as Israel was a holy nation. Just as Israel had broken the vows she had taken to the Lord, so Samson broke every one of his Nazarite vows. He had vowed not to associate with death, yet he killed a lion, and even then ate honey from the carcass a few days later (14:6–9). He had vowed not to drink alcohol, yet he arranged a drinking feast after his first marriage. Perhaps most famously, he didn't keep the vow never to cut his hair. He had married a Philistine woman called Delilah, who was working with the Philistines to kill Samson. Three times she asked Samson the secret of his strength. The first two times he lied, and the Philistines failed to capture him, but finally he was worn down by Delilah and told her the truth: he had vowed not to cut his hair, and if it was cut his strength would leave him.

So Delilah shaved his head while he was asleep, his strength left him, and he was captured by the Philistines. But as he lay in the Philistine prison, his hair began to grow back. Samson was brought into the Philistine temple, where they prepared to sacrifice him to their god Dagon. But Samson prayed for one last feat of strength, and he knocked down the pillars of the temple, killing both himself and all the Philistines who were present (16:30). But even this looks more like petty revenge than doing the Lord's work.

Samson and Delilah by José Echenagusía

Epilogues: Progressive deterioration

The book of Judges represents things getting worse and worse in Israel. This is seen vividly in the last section. Religious corruption is seen in the story of the Levite who sets himself up as a priest for hire, and encourages devotion not to the Lord, but to an idol. This man is a grandson of Moses himself, showing how far the nation has fallen so quickly (18:30).

The religious corruption leads to moral and social corruption, culminating with a gang-rape that mirrors the events in Sodom in Genesis 19. Israel is not a light to the nations; rather Israel has become *like* the nations. These are some of the darkest chapters in all of Scripture. The book closes with words that are repeated numerous times in these chapters: "In those days there was no king in Israel. Everyone did what was right in his own eyes" (21:25, ESV).

LOOKING AHEAD TO JESUS:
The leader we need

This diagnosis of the problem also hints at the solution. A leader is needed who will not die. A king is needed who will restrain the people's evil and deliver them from their enemies. A priest is needed who will not hide away in the face of danger and let women be abused, but who will step out into the darkness to protect his beloved, even if it costs him his life.

Judges is a dark book, but it provides the backdrop against which the glittering beauty of the gospel hope shines.

SAMUEL: THE GIFT OF KINGSHIP

Over one thousand years had passed since the people entered the Promised Land under Joshua. They had known oppression from foreign powers, and the collapse of all religious, moral, and social order. One thousand times the trees had blossomed in spring, but the nation of Israel itself seemed locked in an everlasting winter. Joy and hope were in short supply. All until the Lord gave his people a king...

Naomi entreating Ruth and Orpah by William Blake

God's good plan of kingship

Many people today are nervous of authority. Across the world we see people abusing their power, using it to become rich, to exploit others, and to avoid any accountability. The Bible is unswerving in its condemnation of those who abuse their power, showing the horror of leaders who are self-serving. But although it can be abused, the Bible presents kingship in Israel as a *gift* – so long as a good king is in charge. The Bible story so far has been scattered with indications that the monarchy is coming, and that it was always part of God's good plan to bless his people and the world.

Genesis 1:27–28	Adam had a kingly role.
Genesis 17:16	Sarah was told kings would come from her line.
Genesis 49:8, 10	Judah was promised that his tribe would be the one from whom kings would come.
Deuteronomy 17:14–20	The law already contained instructions on how the king was to live. This law was radical in the ancient world, presenting the king as someone who was to be one of the people and *serve* the people, not be served by them. The king was to read the law and rule under God's authority.
Judges 21:25	The problem in Judges was that there was no king in Israel.

The book of Ruth

The book of Ruth, found in the English Bible between Judges and Samuel, is a beautiful story of God's provision and care for one family. Naomi faced great hardship as she fled her homeland due to famine. Her husband and two sons died while she was in Moab, leaving her poor and vulnerable. She returned home to Bethlehem with her daughter-in-law, Ruth. There, despite Ruth being a foreigner, she was cared for by a righteous man, Boaz. After a tender pastoral romance, they were married, and Ruth and Naomi were provided for.

This little book shows God's care for individuals – the weak and vulnerable in particular. But the ending of the book points ahead to the book of Samuel, giving a genealogy of Ruth's children, culminating in King David. God's individual care for Naomi and Ruth is part of his broader plan to bless the world through his chosen king.

Hannah's song: God lifts up the humble

The book of Samuel begins with a focus on Hannah, who would be the mother of Samuel the prophet. She was unable to bear children – as with so many in Scripture whom God uses greatly – but at the Temple God promised her that she would bear a son. She sang a song of praise to God, and this song sets up the narrative to come, with the emphasis on *reversals*. God opposes the proud but lifts up the humble. The final words of the song speak of the Lord's king: "[God] will give strength to his king and exalt the horn of his anointed" (1 Samuel 2:10). Hannah's song presents kingship in a positive light, but crucially indicates what sort of kingship God requires: not proud, "high", human strength, but humble, lowly dependence on God.

Samuel

Samuel was the last judge of Israel, the one who ushered in the age of the kings. He also represents the beginning of the separation of the roles of king and prophet. The king leads

Shiloh, where the tent of meeting was set up before David moved it to Jerusalem

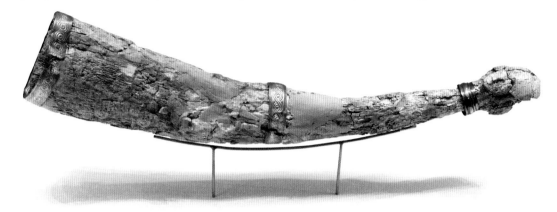

the people, but the prophet – like Samuel – teaches God's law. The prophets were a regular irritation to the kings, preventing them from having too much power, and calling them back to the law of God. It would only be with the coming of Jesus Christ that the roles of prophet and king would come together in the same person.

Saul

Saul was the first of Israel's kings. His role – as with all the kings – was to be God's chosen instrument to save the people from their enemies, and to lead the people in faithful obedience to God (1 Samuel 9:15–17). The prophet marked him out by pouring oil over his head – "anointing" him. This is where we get the words "Messiah" and "Christ" from: they are the Hebrew and Greek words for "anointed". Calling Jesus the "Christ" or "Messiah" means he is the divinely appointed king like in the Old Testament.

The people had asked for a king for sinful reasons – to be like the other nations – and in Saul they receive a king *like* those of the nations. Saul was tall, impressive, and powerful. But he did not honour the Lord. He refused to follow the Lord's commands to completely destroy the Amalekites – not out of pity, but because he was greedy and wanted the best of their livestock for himself. He proved to be like his father Adam in not ridding the garden of the serpent. Moreover, he then set up a monument in *his* own honour – an event which typified his kingship. So the Lord rejected him as king. The presentation of Saul is predominantly negative, to provide a contrast with the next king, David: a king after God's heart.

LOOKING AHEAD TO JESUS:
The Servant King

The humble rule spoken of by Hannah would be seen partially in King David, but would be perfectly fulfilled in Jesus Christ, who came "not to be served, but to serve, and to give his life as a ransom for many" (Mark 10:45). This also sets the pattern for any true Christian leadership: it should not be that of "exercising authority" over others, but serving them in humility.

21 DAVID: THE PERSECUTED MESSIAH

Israel's first king had been a disaster. The Lord told Samuel to anoint a new king, this time from an insignificant town called Bethlehem, and the family of a man named Jesse. When Jesse brings forward his sons, Samuel – who we think might know better by now – assumes that tall, impressive Eliab is the one. But the Lord says no. Jesse presents the rest of his sons, but each time the Lord says no. "Are there any more?" asks Samuel. "Just one," is the answer. "The youngest and smallest. We didn't even think to bring him, he's off tending the sheep..."

Slingshots are still used today by Berber shepherds to drive away wild animals

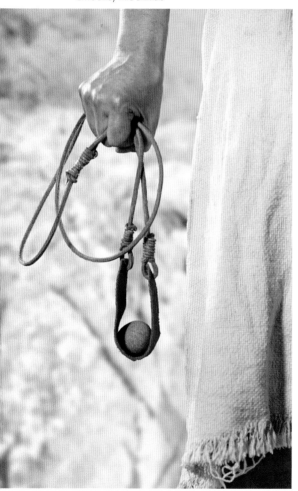

The Lord looks at the heart

In choosing David to be king, the Lord fulfils Hannah's words: he opposes the proud and lifts up the humble. "People look at the outward appearance, but the LORD looks at the heart" (1 Samuel 16:7). In this way David foreshadows Jesus Christ: "He had no beauty or majesty to attract us to him, nothing in his appearance that we should desire him" (Isaiah 53:2). David is not impressive in human terms, but he is a man after God's own heart, and is empowered by the Spirit of God.

David and Goliath

The people of Israel were under attack from the Philistines, and their champion, the giant Goliath, challenged anyone to face him, but no one would. David heard of this and volunteered to fight Goliath, defeating him with only the help of his sling and stones. This is far more than just a story about how small people can win big victories. Goliath is described as an enemy of God, and his armour with its "scales" is reminiscent of the serpent in the Garden of Eden. He is an offspring of the serpent, attacking God's people. Saul, as the king, was supposed to accept the champion's challenge. Like Adam before him, he was supposed to put his own life on the line in order to defeat the serpent. But, like Adam, he failed.

David saved his people, without them having to even fight. He is the one who slays the serpent – cutting off Goliath's head (compare to Genesis 3:15). The message of the story is that God is keeping his promises to deliver his people through a king.

The suffering Messiah

Despite having been anointed as king, and despite this great victory over Goliath, for much of the books of Samuel, David is not on the throne, but on the run. Saul remains as king, and devotes his energy to killing David. David is found hiding out in caves, betrayed by friends, having no permanent abode. Many of the psalms reflect his difficult experiences during this time. David is setting the pattern for a suffering Messiah. These are surely some of the accounts that Jesus referenced when, on the road to Emmaus, he explained to his disciples from the Scriptures that he, the Messiah, had to "suffer these things" before entering his glory (Luke 24:26).

The covenant with David

When David was finally installed as king, he completed the conquest that had stuttered in the time of the judges. He brought rest to the people and the land (2 Samuel 7:1).

Osmar Schindler's depiction of David facing Goliath

He made Jerusalem his capital, and brought the ark of God to the city, so that once again God could dwell in the midst of his people. David wanted to build a Temple – a "house" for the Lord, but instead the Lord said that he would build a "house" – meaning a dynasty – for David. God promised David a son, who would build the Temple for God. This son would not just be David's son, he would be known as God's son. His kingdom would endure forever.

The language echoes that of the covenant with Abraham: a "great name"; promise of land, people, and blessing (2 Samuel 7:9–10). God will fulfil his promises to Abraham through a king – Messiah – from David's line. Previously in the story, a faithful Israel was needed for God's promises to be fulfilled. Now this is narrowed down to one man: what is needed is a faithful king. The king will carry the fortunes of the nation.

This promise is partially fulfilled in Solomon, David's son, who builds the Temple. But the glorious robes of these promises ultimately prove too large for Solomon – or any of the kings who follow – and only truly fit David's greater son, Jesus.

Decline and end

The reigns of David and Saul are full of contradictions. The role of the king is presented in such positive terms, yet the reality is so far short of this. Saul shows the failure and dangers of human kingship, but even David is far from universally positive. Towards the end of the book David was on his rooftop, from where he could see a woman bathing, whose name was Bathsheba. He saw her, he wanted her, and so he took her. He then added murder to this, as he had the woman's husband Uriah killed and took her as his wife (2 Samuel 11:1–27). He is abusing his power, and acting like Saul or even Pharaoh. The book ends with David facing God's judgment for another sin – taking a census and so trusting in his own military might, not the Lord.

LOOKING AHEAD TO JESUS:
The faithful king

At his best, David is a picture of Jesus, the Messiah to come. Jesus came to defeat his people's greatest enemy, without them having to lift a finger. But at his worst, David acts as a negative foil, showing that no human, sinful king could ever lead the people properly into the blessings of God. The narrative drives us to look for a king who will always be faithful, who will never use his power to oppress the weak.

The Moabite stone, dating from 840 BC, is possibly the earliest extra-biblical reference to the kingdom of Israel and the "house of David"

PSALMS: PRAYERS FOR ALL SEASONS

Until David, music rarely featured in Israelite worship, but with the installation of David as king in Jerusalem, the worship of God's people exploded into song. The book of Psalms was the hymn book of ancient Israel, used by God's people as they gathered in worship. The original Hebrew title was "Praises", but in fact there are three main types of psalm: praise, thanksgiving, and lament. Perhaps the title "Praises" indicates that true praise of God goes beyond the bold, upbeat statements of celebration, but also encompasses much harder situations, the sort of praise that trusts God even in the midst of great trials.

The psalms are honest about the hardships that Christians may endure

Psalms of lament

To lament is to cry out to God in a time of distress. The psalmists pour out their hearts with great emotion. "How long, O Lord?" (ESV) is a characteristic way for a lament to begin. The range of things that the psalmists lament about is extraordinary: enemies, sickness, those who attack their reputation, suffering, loneliness, even God being distant.

Typical structure of a lament psalm (e.g. Psalm 13)
An address to God – e.g. "O Lord" (NLT).
Telling God the problem.
Asking God to act.
Affirmation of trust, and promise to praise when deliverance comes.

In contrast to the way many Christians pray today, the psalmists spend far longer telling God the problem than telling him what to do about it. The psalmists describe the situation in great detail, and also how it feels, before simply asking God to *act*. This means that even in situations where the psalmist can't imagine what a good outcome of the situation might be (i.e. not know what to pray for) the psalmist can still pray.

Rawness and authenticity

The way the psalmists speak is significant also. There is a rawness to their speech. But it is framed by the address: "O Lord". To lament is different from grumbling *about* God. A characteristic word is "you", as the psalmists bring their distress *to* God. Also, the lament psalms tend to finish with an affirmation of trust – yet this does not cancel out the reality of the sorrow and questions expressed earlier on. These psalms teach that sometimes the only right response to a situation is weeping, and that questions and tears are not incompatible with resolute trust in God.

Psalms of praise

Typical structure of a praise psalm (e.g. Psalm 113)
Call to praise.
Reasons given (character and deeds of God).

Praise psalms always give reasons for praise: who the Lord is, and what he has done. A characteristic word in them is "he", as the psalmist speaks *about* the Lord. The psalms have a rich doctrine of God; it's one of the reasons Martin Luther called them "the little Bible". These psalms were not simply meant to express, but *shape* the spiritual experiences and emotions of the singers. Meditation on who the Lord is and what he has done is what lifts a Christian's heart to praise the Lord.

Psalms of thanksgiving

Psalms of thanksgiving have a more personal focus than the praise psalms, expressing thanks to God for a particular deliverance. A characteristic word is "I", as the psalmist speaks of their own experience of distress, and how the Lord answered them. These psalms are important because they show the need to remember deliverances, and thank God for them. Throughout Israel's history, disaster always looms when the people forget what the Lord has done for them.

Women raise their hands in worship to God

Typical structure of a thanksgiving psalm (e.g. Psalm 116)
Narrative of distress.
Account of the Lord's deliverance.
Praise to God and call for others to join in the praise.

The praise and thanksgiving psalms not only express emotion, but also shape it. Regularly using the thanksgiving psalms would have shaped the people into being those who saw every blessing as coming from the Lord. It would also have prepared the people to expect that every distress can be faced by looking to the Lord, who had delivered them in the past.

In these psalms, the singers readily mingle national deliverances – such as redemption from Egypt – with more personal deliverances, perhaps from an illness. The fact that the Lord delivered in the "big" situations of need is a cause to think he will deliver in more personal distress. Conversely, every personal deliverance becomes an opportunity to celebrate the larger deliverances – and the character of the Lord who is a deliverer.

King David plays the harp in the *Bible Historiale*

LOOKING AHEAD TO JESUS:
Christ in the psalms

The psalms take on even greater meaning in the light of the coming of Christ. He may be seen in different (and sometimes overlapping) ways in the psalms:

Christ as the singer of the psalms. The laments speak of the sufferings of Christ.	*e.g. "How long must I wrestle with my thoughts and day after day have sorrow in my heart?" (Psalm 13:2).*
Christ as the king – especially in the "royal" psalms (Psalms 2; 18; 20; 21; 45; 72; 101; 110; 132; 144).	*e.g. "In your majesty ride forth victoriously in the cause of truth, humility and justice; let your right hand achieve awesome deeds" (Psalm 45:4).*
Christ as the Lord of whom the psalm speaks.	*e.g. "The LORD is my shepherd" (Psalm 23:1).*
Christ as the saviour – all the little deliverances in the psalms point to Christ's big deliverance won at the cross.	*e.g. "He lifted me out of the slimy pit, out of the mud and mire" (Psalm 40:2).*

Christians today can use the psalms to praise, thank, and lament, just as the Israelites would have done, and can do so all the more as they see Christ's majesty, suffering, and salvation foretold.

SOLOMON: PRINCE OF PEACE

Jerusalem in Solomon's day would have been a feast for the senses. Everywhere you looked, a new wonder, brought from distant lands by the trading ships. The many languages of the traders and visiting dignitaries would mingle with the music of the many instruments and the vast Temple choir. New sights, new tastes, new smells on every side, as caravans from the East brought exotic spices and finery. One's eyes would linger on the intricately carved wood and brightly coloured fine cloth of Solomon's royal palace. And the gold. So much gold that silver was considered of little value; so much gold overlaid on the wall of the Temple that it was said when the sun rose it looked as if the whole mountain were on fire.

A range of exotic spices from the Middle East

The kingdom of God

The accounts of Solomon, King David's son, present kingship at its best. A son of Adam ruling as Adam should have, filling and subduing the earth. This is a picture of the kingdom of God, in all its prosperity, wisdom, and peace. The world as it should have been, and will be: a foreshadowing of the glories to come in the new heavens and the new earth.

Wisdom

One night God appeared to Solomon and said he would grant any request. Instead of asking for wealth, riches, or honour, Solomon asked for *wisdom* so that he might govern God's people rightly. Wisdom, according to Scripture, is not so much about knowledge as about *living rightly*. This has a spiritual dimension: "The fear of the LORD is the beginning of wisdom" (Proverbs 9:10), which has very varied and practical outworkings. Solomon wrote songs, spoke proverbs, classified plants, created infrastructure, governed with justice, promoted architecture, and both learned from and blessed the nations around. Such was his wisdom and fame that the Queen of Sheba came to listen to him, and marvelled at how wonderful it must be to live with such a wise king: "How happy your people must be! How happy your officials, who continually stand before you and hear your wisdom!" (2 Chronicles 9:7).

The vine is a biblical symbol of joy and abundance

Prosperity for the people

Under Solomon, the people enjoyed a level of peace and prosperity that they had never known before. Freed from war, and with a flourishing economy, everyone was able to enjoy life "under their own vine and under their own fig tree" (1 Kings 4:25), which has Eden-like connotations of rest and satisfaction: "The people of Judah and Israel were as numerous as the sand on the seashore; they ate, they drank and they were happy" (1 Kings 4:20). Just as Abraham had been promised – a great nation, in their Promised Land, enjoying *blessing*. This was God's kingdom at its best in the Old Testament, though it was still relatively local: blessing had not gone to all the nations as had been promised to Abraham in Genesis 12:1–3. Eden had not been extended to encompass the whole earth, as God had always intended.

Temple

Now the people were settled in their Promised Land, David wanted to build a Temple – a permanent dwelling place for God – to replace the movable tabernacle. The Lord permitted David to make the preparations for the building of the Temple, but David had shed too much blood in war to be the Temple builder. And so it was his son Solomon of whom the Lord said, "He is the one who will build a house for my Name. He will be my son, and I will be his father. And I will establish the throne of his kingdom over Israel for ever" (1 Chronicles 22:10).

Solomon took seven years to build the Temple, and filled it with gold, beautifully carved wood in the shape of flowers, and precious stones. The significance of these was more than just their beauty. They are echoes of Eden: the Temple is a mini-paradise where God will dwell amongst his people, and from which blessing will go to the world.

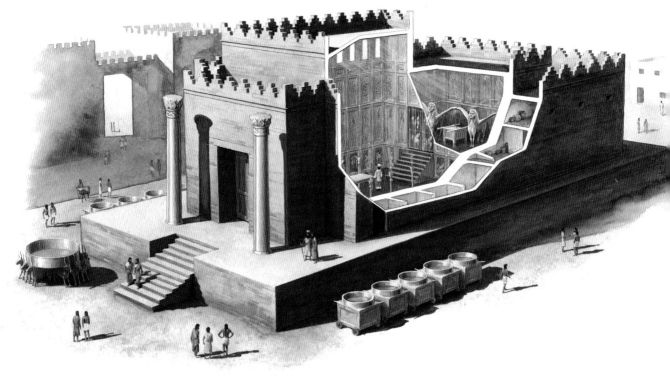

A possible reconstruction of Solomon's Temple at Jerusalem

LOOKING AHEAD TO JESUS:
One greater than Solomon

Under the early years of Solomon's reign, Israel saw the best of kingship. They knew peace, prosperity, and the joy of having a wise king, with God in their midst. This was the golden age, with a new Adam ruling in a new Eden. This is a mini-picture of the kingdom of God, of what life was intended to be.

This is the background against which the New Testament announcement "Jesus is king" must be understood. The hearts' cry of later generations of Old Testament Israelites would have been, "If only we had a king like Solomon! If only we had a kingdom like that again!" Jesus being the king meant he was the one to bring about days like these again. But Solomon's kingdom, glorious though it was, is only a pale shadow of the greater glories of Christ's kingdom to come. Jesus was like Solomon – but so much greater than Solomon (Matthew 12:42). The kingdom of Solomon was intended to make God's people imagine the greater glories of Christ's coming kingdom. If the "shadow" was as glorious as Jerusalem under Solomon, how much more glorious would the reality be. Greater peace, greater prosperity, greater art and music, greater scientific endeavour, greater unity, greater joy! This is the kingdom that Christ's people enter and experience in part in this life, but fully and completely when Christ returns (see p. 160–62).

24 WISDOM LITERATURE 1: THE ORDER OF EDEN

Solomon was famous for his wisdom. On one occasion two women came to him, both claiming to be the mother of a certain baby. Solomon proposed the baby be cut in two and half given to each. One woman agreed, but the other refused and said the child should be given to the other. Solomon thus revealed the true mother – the one who would rather lose her baby than any harm come to it. This incident shows that wisdom is about more than just knowledge and information. Solomon's wisdom encompassed all areas of life, and is recorded in the "wisdom books" of Proverbs, Ecclesiastes, and Song of Songs. Along with the book of Job, they do not advance the storyline of Scripture, but sit alongside the story, giving truths of life for all times, places, and peoples.

Proverbs: The order of Eden

The book of Proverbs is addressed by King Solomon to his son, perhaps to train the prince in the wisdom he will need as king. These are not primarily commands to be followed, but general observations of how the world works, and encouragements to live in the light of wisdom. At one level, the wisdom in Proverbs mirrors other ancient wisdom traditions, and even wisdom today. The book is full of characters whom we recognize: the sluggard, the foolish youth, the neighbour who comes round and stays too long. Most of the teaching comprises observations about daily life in the world God created: work, money, friendships, marriage, speech, government. One writer described it as "godliness in working clothes".[8] Yet God is not absent from the book; the introduction lays the foundation on which everything else is built: "The fear of the LORD is the beginning of knowledge" (Proverbs 1:7).

Is Proverbs naive?

But is Proverbs naive? "The righteous eat to their hearts' content, but the stomach of the wicked goes hungry" (13:25). Surely this is not always the case. There are plenty of righteous people who suffer hunger.

The answer is twofold: first, these are not promises, but generalizations to live by. The book of Proverbs itself suggests this reading strategy. The first part of the book contains more general principles that seem quite black and white, but then the book moves to consider more complex situations. Sometimes different principles will be in conflict with each other, and

Daily life in the Middle East today

Gustave Moreau's watercolour illustration of the Song of Songs

so the reader must meditate and reflect on which applies in each case. Just two verses before the proverb quoted above is another that prevents it being understood too woodenly: "An unploughed field produces food for the poor, but injustice sweeps it away" (13:23).

Second, some proverbs point forward to how life *should be* and one day will be. The order reflected in Proverbs teaches Christians to live now, but also orients them to the better future they await, when Solomon's greater son will reign in perfect wisdom and justice and the righteous *will* eat to their hearts' content.

Song of Songs

The Song of Songs is a series of sublime love songs between the king and his bride, the Shulamite woman. Many have seen a narrative through the songs, beginning with the longing of the early songs, moving through the marriage of the two lovers, to celebration of the sexual intimacy between them in later songs. Yet this is no straightforward progression – even after the consummation there are times of frustration and alienation between the man and the woman.

There is a frank openness about erotic love in the song, right from the very first words: "Let him kiss me with the kisses of his mouth"

(1:2). Both the lovers praise each other for their physical beauty: "His arms are rods of gold set with topaz. His body is like polished ivory decorated with lapis lazuli" (5:14); "Your breasts are like two fawns, like twin fawns of a gazelle that browse among the lilies" (4:5). Sex is not seen as something dirty or shameful, but rather seen as a wonderful gift of God in creation. The context for sex is marriage, and by extolling the virtues of sex within marriage, the song also warns against the dangers of lust and infidelity (8:6). The song is extremely sensuous, yet not voyeuristic; sexual intimacy is described, but in metaphorical terms: "Let my beloved come to his garden and taste its choice fruits" (4:16).

Jesus is often depicted as a bridegroom in art

LOOKING AHEAD TO JESUS:
Jesus the bridegroom

The frank celebration of sex has led some commentators to see the song soley as an allegory of Christ's relationship for his church, not a description of human marriage and sexuality. Others see the book as purely about human relationships, with little to say about God. In Scripture, God's relationship with his people is repeatedly described as a marriage relationship. This means the song can be both: a celebration of romantic love, and a picture of the intense and powerful love between Christ and his church.

The language of the book is consistently reminiscent of Eden: garden language, jewels, and splendour. The song speaks of the troubles of marriage, yet also of the fact that, at its best, marriage is a picture of the way God intended the universe to be. The song ultimately speaks of Jesus the king who will pass through great difficulties to pursue his bride, to make her beautiful, and to return her to lush vineyards, places of springs. The Song celebrates human marriage, but it doesn't make it ultimate. It points to the greater marriage to come, and to the lover whose love is not just "strong as death" (8:6) but stronger, enduring even beyond the grave.

WISDOM LITERATURE 2: THE DISORDER OF THE FALL

Proverbs and Song of Songs reflect a view of the world from the perspective of creation. By contrast, Ecclesiastes and Job have the perspective of the world being *fallen*; that everyone now lives "east of Eden". Ecclesiastes is a frank meditation on how life is confusing, disappointing, and frustrating; Job records the deep sufferings of an innocent man. These books are an important foil for the generally positive and certain message of Proverbs and Song of Songs.

Life can appear like fog – often complicated and difficult to understand

Ecclesiastes: Life east of Eden

Ecclesiastes teaches that life is fleeting and hard to understand. This is captured in a Hebrew word used thirty-seven times into the book: *hebel*. Often translated as "meaningless" or "vanity", it literally means "breath" or "vapour". It is the same word as the name "Abel" from Genesis 4, the first man to be murdered. The apostle Paul uses the equivalent Greek word when he is describing how the world is fallen and now subject to "frustration" (Romans 8:20). *Hebel* describes what life is like east of Eden.

| Everything is breath (*hebel*) | **Things don't last.** Like breath which quickly disappears, like Abel whose life was so quickly and tragically cut short, we all live with the shadow of death looming over us. |
| 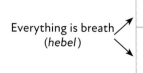 | **Things are hard to understand.** Just as you can't catch hold of breath, so you can't quite understand the world. Just when you think you have things worked out, it escapes you again, like chasing after the wind (Ecclesiastes 1:14). |

A pessimistic book?

The message of Ecclesiastes may seem quite pessimistic. It candidly describes what life is like in a fallen world, and reminds us of our creatureliness. It is a caution to those believers who think they have everything sorted out, and want life to be neat and tidy.

Yet this then allows for the positive message of the book: "So I commend the enjoyment of life, because there is nothing better for a person under the sun than to eat and drink and be glad. Then joy will accompany them in their toil all the days of the life God has given them under the sun" (8:15). It also encourages Christians to long for the return of Christ, when the *hebel* (frustration/meaninglessness/vanity) of life "under the sun" will end, as God's people return to Eden, eternal life, and the unclouded blessings of God.

Job

The book of Job concerns a rich man who was righteous and feared the Lord. In the opening scene, God permits Satan to afflict Job: first he loses his wealth, then he suffers the death of his children, and finally he is afflicted with serious illness. Satan thinks this will lead Job to curse God, but Job does not sin by charging God with wrongdoing.

Leon Bonnat's representation of Job

The main section of the book contains cycles of speeches between Job and his friends. The friends first sit with Job for seven days in dust and ashes, to grieve with him. When they do speak, they exhibit a simplistic view of how God works: they assume God rewards the righteous and punishes the wicked, and so tell Job his suffering must be due to his having sinned. In Job's answers, he continues to lament his suffering, rebukes his friends for their unhelpful words, and demands an audience with God himself to sort things out.

At the end of the book of Job, God speaks out of a storm

The Lord's speeches

We might expect, therefore, that the book ends in a way that matches the beginning – with Job being taken up to the heavenly court to see "behind the scenes" what has been going on, and learning that his suffering has been a test. But instead, the book ends with the Lord speaking out of a storm:

> *Where were you when I laid*
> *the earth's foundation?*
> *Tell me, if you understand.*

Job 38:4

God speaks of his creation power and wisdom, in contrast to Job's limited knowledge. The Lord then speaks of his power over two terrifying monsters, Behemoth and Leviathan, which are representations of death and evil. The Lord is sovereign even over these powerful and incomprehensible enemies.

 LOOKING AHEAD TO JESUS:
God with us

The ending of Job points to the incarnation, when God became flesh in Jesus Christ. God came to live in a world of suffering and evil – and more than that, to die to put an end to suffering and evil. There is a perfect happy ending coming when Christ returns, and until then, Jesus promises to be with his people always, even in a painful and perplexing world. Jesus is "Immanuel" – God with us.

The ending of Job

The book ends with God vindicating Job, restoring his property, and giving him a new family. Job never got *answers* for why he was suffering. But he got an encounter with God himself, and that was enough. God's people of all ages will suffer, often when they have done nothing wrong. Like Job, they shouldn't expect to be given a view of all God's purposes in their suffering, but they should expect God to be with them.

26

THE KINGDOM SPLITS: GOD'S JUDGMENT FALLS

The kingdom reached its high point under Solomon – the golden age of peace and prosperity. But Solomon's heart turned away from the Lord as he took foreign wives and worshipped their foreign gods. Peace gave way to conflict, prosperity turned to uncertainty, and the kingdom was torn in two. God had not abandoned his people, rather this was what God had always promised: obedience would lead to blessing, but disobedience would lead to judgment.

The kingdom splits

Solomon started off well, but by the end of his reign he had broken all the laws given to the king (Deuteronomy 17:14–20). He had amassed for himself horses from Egypt. He had taken many foreign wives, and along with them many foreign gods. He had hoarded excessive silver and gold. Most importantly, he had disregarded the law of God. Idolatry entered the land through Solomon, and he led the people astray.

As a result the Lord judged him. When he died, his son Rehoboam took the throne, but quickly ten of the twelve tribes rebelled and made Jeroboam, one of Solomon's officials, king over them. Thus the kingdom of Israel was divided. The southern kingdom was loyal to Rehoboam, and was comprised of the tribes of Judah and Benjamin. From here on this is known simply as "Judah". The northern kingdom comprising the other ten tribes followed Jeroboam, and kept the name "Israel".

The sin of Jeroboam: The golden calves

Jeroboam was concerned that the people from his northern kingdom would want to travel to the southern kingdom, to Jerusalem, to worship in the Temple. This might undermine their loyalty to him. So he set up golden calves at Dan and Bethel – places of worship at the northern and southern edges of his kingdom. Just as Aaron had done with the golden calf at Mount Sinai, Jeroboam replaced worship of the true God with worship of idols: "Here

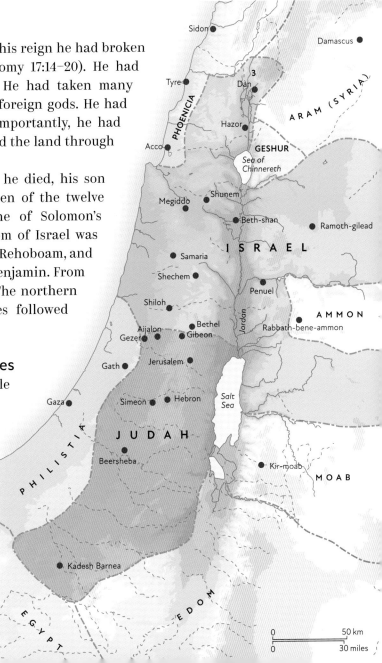

God promised his people that if they were unfaithful they would be uprooted like a tree

are your gods, Israel, who brought you up out of Egypt" (1 Kings 12:28). This was a self-made religion, one which turned people's hearts away from the Lord, yet he framed it in terms that had some history, so as to give some air of legitimacy to what he was doing. It felt ancient, it felt religious, yet it was a rebellion against the Lord and a direct transgression of both the first and second Commandments.

The northern kings following Jeroboam

The Lord sent a prophet, Ahijah, to Jeroboam to confront him for his sin. Ahijah declared that because of Jeroboam's sin, "The LORD will strike Israel as a reed is shaken in the water, and root up Israel out of this good land that he gave to their fathers and scatter them beyond the Euphrates" (1 Kings 14:15).

The rest of the history of Israel would be a working out of this prophecy. Israel, and also its king, was like a reed in water – precarious and unstable. There were assassinations, rebellions, and a succession of different royal dynasties in Israel, none of them lasting very long.

This is *prophetic* history, giving God's perspective on the important events. The narrative focuses on the kings, as God's covenant is now tied to the kings. The wellbeing of the people depends on the faithfulness of the king. Yet the repeated summary statement for the kings of Israel is that they "did evil in the eyes of the LORD, following the ways of Jeroboam and committing the same sin Jeroboam had caused Israel to commit" (1 Kings 15:34).

The southern kingdom – high places

The book of Kings intersperses the history of the northern kingdom with that of Judah in the south. While the northern kings were all evil, in Judah things were somewhat better. After Rehoboam and Abijah, Asa was a good king, who did right in the eyes of the Lord, as his ancestor David had done. But he – as with so many kings after him – was not wholehearted in his obedience. He left the "high places" in the land. These were places of worship, but not the place God had appointed: the Temple in Jerusalem. This was not the worship of different gods, as happened in the northern kingdom. This was worship of the Lord, but in the wrong place and in the wrong way. The whole Bible is the story of the quest for the return to the "holy mountain" of Eden, but along the way there are many counterfeits. Like the tower of Babel, these "high places" were an attempt to reach God on the people's own terms – and significantly these "high places" became places of sexual immorality and ungodliness, in contrast to the holiness that was required to ascend the true hill of the Lord (Psalm 24:3–4).

LOOKING AHEAD TO JESUS:
Unity

Just as in Eden, sin led to conflict and division. Without God honoured as king, people sought status for themselves, often at the expense of others. The northern and southern kingdoms were not simply divided, they were often at war.

In Christ, all things would be put back together again. Christ would bring unity between those of different backgrounds and different races. The apostle Paul speaks of how God "made known to us the mystery of his will according to his good pleasure, which he purposed in Christ, to be put into effect when the times reach their fulfilment – to bring unity to all things in heaven and on earth under Christ" (Ephesians 1:9–10).

The Kings of Judah and Isreal

JUDAH	ISRAEL
Rehoboam 930–913	Jeroboam 930–909
Abijah 913–910	
Asa 910–869	Nadab 909–908
	Baasha 908–886
	Elah 886–885
	Zimri 885
	Tibni 885–880
	Omri 880–874
	Ahab 874–853
Jehoshaphat 872–848	
	Ahaziah 853–852
	Joram 852–841
Jehoram 848–841	
Ahaziah 841	Jehu 841–814
Athaliah 841–835	
Joash 835–796	
	Jehoahaz 814–798
	Jehoash 798–782
Amaziah 796–767	
	Jeroboam II 793–753
Azariah (Uzziah) 792/767–740	
	Zechariah 753
	Shallum 752
	Menahem 752–742
	Pekahiah 742–740
	Pekah 752–732
Jotham 750/40–735	
Ahaz 735–715	
	Hoshea 732–722
Hezekiah 715–686	
Manasseh 697–642	
Amon 642–640	
Josiah 640–609	
Jehoahaz 609	
Jehoiakim 609–598	*N.B. Where dates overlap,*
Jehoiachin 598–597	*this indicates a co-regency*
Zedekiah 597–586	

ELIJAH AND ELISHA: GOD'S PATIENCE

The stories of the prophets Elijah and Elisha are among the most surprising in all the Bible (1 Kings 17 – 2 Kings 8). The fast-paced history slows right down to focus on some extraordinary events in Ahab's reign. First, there are the miracles: floating axe heads, fire from the sky, chariots and horsemen of fire, the raising of the dead. Even in the Bible, such events are unusual. More surprising, though, is that the prophets Elijah and Elisha appear at all. Ahab is ruling the northern kingdom, and he does more evil than all the kings before him. Yet rather than judging him straight away, the Lord gives him chance after chance after chance…

The land of Israel was prone to drought

Evil King Ahab

Ahab was more wicked than all the kings who preceded him. He and his wife Jezebel promoted the immoral worship of the Canaanite gods Baal and Asherah. They tried to kill all of God's prophets – demonstrating themselves to be "offspring of the serpent" figures (see p. 20). In their days, worship of the Lord had almost been abandoned.

Elijah, like all the prophets who would succeed him, called the people back to the covenant. He predicted the covenant curse of famine on the land due to lack of rain, which is what happened (1 Kings 17:1–7). This was a particularly appropriate judgment on Ahab's Baal worship, as Baal was supposed to be the fertility god who sent the rains that the land so desperately needed each year.

Elijah and the prophets of Baal

The story could have ended there, but there was salvation beyond this judgment. Elijah organized a "god-contest" on Mount Carmel. Both he and the prophets of Baal were to build altars, and the god who sent fire would be seen to be the true God. The prophets of Baal went first, and despite crying out all day, dancing round the altar, and even cutting themselves until their blood flowed, there was no answer.

Then Elijah stepped forward, and, having drenched his altar in water to make the job even harder, he prayed to the Lord: "Answer me, LORD, answer me, so these people will know that you, LORD, are God, and that you are turning their hearts back again" (1 Kings 18:37). The Lord answered by sending fire from heaven – proving he was the true God, but also showing he accepted the sacrifice and still wanted relationship with his people.

Elijah on the run

Elijah enjoyed a great victory, but just moments later he was on the run again, chased by Jezebel, who wanted to kill him. Elijah was despondent and wanted to give up – even wanted to die. But God sent an angel to sustain him with food.

Elijah met the Lord at Mount Sinai, in a very similar way to how Moses had before him. The Lord promised that judgment would fall on Ahab, but also that Elijah was not the only faithful one left: God had reserved a remnant of 7,000 who had not bowed down to Baal. Despite how bleak things seemed, God's covenant promises were on track.

Elisha – the new Joshua

Just as Moses had been succeeded by Joshua, so Elijah was succeeded by Elisha. At the end of his life, Elijah was taken into heaven with chariots of fire and a whirlwind, leaving his cloak behind for his assistant Elisha as a symbol of his authority (2 Kings 2).

Elisha did many similar miracles to Elijah. Like Elijah, he struck the Jordan river with his cloak, and it was parted – also reminiscent of Moses leading the people out of Egypt through the Red Sea, and Joshua leading the people into the Promised Land through the Jordan.

Like Elijah, Elisha was miraculously fed, provided food for a widow, and raised a woman's son from the dead. However, while Elijah was known for national events – condemning King Ahab, and calling for national repentance – Elisha had a more personal ministry, purifying a deadly stew, multiplying loaves of barley to provide food for a hundred men, recovering a lost axe head (essentially someone's livelihood), and curing Naaman of leprosy.

A Russian icon from c. 1290 shows Elijah ascending to heaven

LOOKING AHEAD TO JESUS:
Light in the darkness

Elijah and Elisha foreshadow the ministry of John the Baptist and Jesus. The prophet Malachi promised that before the Messiah came, Elijah would first come to turn the people back in repentance, as he had done in Ahab's day. John the Baptist was this "Elijah figure" who preached a message of repentance. Elisha points to the ministry of Jesus: cleansing a leprosy sufferer, transforming water, raising the dead, multiplying food, and giving sight to the blind. Not simply demonstrations of power, but of care for people, of power used for the good of those in great distress. Like Elijah and Elisha, Jesus brought light in a time of great darkness, shone hope where none could be expected, and demonstrated that the Lord was God, and that he still cared for a rebellious and wicked world.

THE EXILE: THE DEATH OF THE NATION

The final years of Israel's history take place under the looming shadow of the Lord's words in Deuteronomy: if the people are not faithful to the covenant, "The LORD will drive you and the king you set over you to a nation unknown to you or your ancestors" (Deuteronomy 28:36). Through the rise and fall of kings, two refrains sound like a death-knell: the northern kings "did evil in the eyes of the LORD by following the sins of Jeroboam" (2 Kings 13:2). The southern kings did not remove the high places. With such repeated rebellion, it could not be long before the people were cast out of their garden-land, as Adam had been so many years before...

The end of the northern kingdom

At this time, the rising superpower in the region was Assyria to the East. In 725 BC, the Assyrian army attacked Samaria, the capital of Israel. Samaria was captured, and the king and many of the people were taken into exile in Assyria. Unusually for Old Testament narrative, which often leaves the interpretation of events to the reader to work out, here the narrator is very explicit about why this happened:

> *All this took place because the Israelites had sinned against the LORD their God, who had brought them up out of Egypt from under the power of Pharaoh, king of Egypt. They worshiped other gods and followed the practices of the nations the LORD had driven out before them...*

2 Kings 17:7–8

Bronze decorations from the great door of the Palace of Shalmaneser III in Balawat, depicting the Assyrian king inspecting prisoners from a conquered city

The king of Assyria then resettled Samaria with people from Assyria, leading to worship in Samaria being a mix of worship of the Lord, but also every other god that the different people brought with them (2 Kings 17:33). This signalled the end of the northern kingdom, as there was no return from the Assyrian exile.

Hezekiah and the siege of Jerusalem

Judah had some faithful kings, so the decline was slower – Judah lasted over 100 years longer than the northern kingdom. King Hezekiah trusted the Lord more than all the kings before him (2 Kings 18:5–7). He removed the high places and led the people in faithfulness to the Lord. With such a good king, things were well within Judah, but Assyria was still seeking to expand its territory, and so Sennacherib, king of Assyria, attacked Judah. The Assyrians captured the fortified towns and reached Jerusalem. There they called out to the people of Judah to surrender. The Assyrian army commander repeatedly urged the people not to trust in God: "Do not let Hezekiah persuade you to trust in the Lord when he says, 'The Lord will surely deliver us; this city will not be given into the hand of the king of Assyria'" (2 Kings 18:30).

Hezekiah's response was to turn to the Lord in prayer. That night the Lord struck down the Assyrians and Jerusalem was spared.

The Jerusalem Prism contains the record of Assyrian King Sennacherib's attacks on Judah and the siege of Jerusalem in the days of Hezekiah. The annals detail cities in Judah that were captured, but significantly Jerusalem is not among them

Manasseh and Josiah

Yet after Hezekiah, his son Manasseh took the throne, who was the most wicked king of Judah. He restored the high places, and promoted the worship of foreign gods, including burning his own son as a sacrifice to one of them. Under his leadership the people "did more evil than the nations the Lord had destroyed before the Israelites" (2 Kings 21:9). Because of Manasseh's sin, the Lord determined that Judah, like Israel before it, would be judged and sent into exile.

There was a brief reprise under the good king Josiah, in whose day the book of the law was rediscovered in the Temple. Josiah read this book – possibly the book of Deuteronomy – and saw how far from God's ways his people had turned. Josiah oversaw great reforms: rebuilding the Temple, removing the high places and foreign gods, even celebrating Passover, which had not

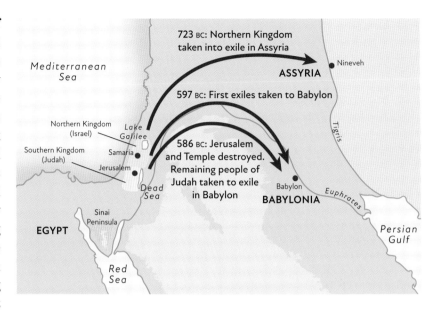

been celebrated like this since the days of the judges. There was no king like Josiah, who turned to the Lord with all his might. But by now it was too late: God had already determined that the sin of Manasseh was too great and that Judah would be taken into exile.

The last days of the southern kingdom

All four kings following Josiah were unfaithful to the Lord, leading to various attacks by foreign powers and deportations – "in accordance with the word of the LORD proclaimed by his servants the prophets" (2 Kings 24:2). By this stage in history, Babylon had replaced Assyria as the great superpower in the East, and in the reign of Jehoiakim, King Nebuchadnezzar of Babylon attacked Jerusalem (2 Kings 24:1). In 597 BC, Jerusalem was captured, and the officials and nobles were exiled to Babylon. Ten years later, Jerusalem and the Temple were completely destroyed, and the remaining people were taken into exile.

LOOKING AHEAD TO JESUS:
The problem of exile

The exile is the great problem that Christ needs to solve. The exile is about so much more than geography or politics. The Promised Land was the place where the people met with God. It had the Temple at its heart, where God had set his name, and promised to hear his people's prayers. Yet the people were cast out of their garden land into exile to the East – they were "removed from [God's] presence" (2 Kings 17:23).

The story has progressed so far, across so many centuries, yet humanity remains "east of Eden", out of relationship with God. The promises to Abraham of a people, land, and blessing now seem a distant memory. Israel has died, and what is needed is nothing less than resurrection. The people need to be brought back from exile, not just into the land, but into the paradise and blessing of God – and the one who will do that is Jesus.

THE PROPHETS: GOD'S MOUTHPIECES

The prophets were raw, confrontational figures, who made national news and gave sleepless nights to kings. They confronted the hypocrisy of the political and religious establishment. They cried out for religious purity and social justice. They didn't look for fame or popularity. Ezekiel lived out the message he preached, and near-starved himself as he acted out the siege of Jerusalem. Jeremiah was flogged, beaten, and thrown in a pit to die. Amos faced deportation from his homeland. Yet in these raw and earthy prophecies are some of the brightest jewels of hope found in the whole Old Testament...

What is a prophet?

Prophets spoke God's words to the people. They stood "in the council of the LORD to see or to hear his word" (Jeremiah 23:18) and then declared that message to the people. The prophets were not primarily "foretelling" the future, though this did happen on some occasions, for example predicting the coming Messiah. The prophets' message was deeply rooted in history and in the covenant God had made with his people. The prophets called for faithfulness to the covenant, giving divinely inspired application of God's word to the current generation. The key themes of the prophets are already found in Deuteronomy:

The prophet Malachi painted by Duccio di Buoninsegna between 1308 and 1311

- There would be blessings if the people obeyed, but curses if they disobeyed.
- They would disobey and be cast out of their land, into exile.
- There was hope beyond judgment, when the Lord would bring them back to their land.

Sin and judgment

The prophets ministered in the days of the decline of Israel and Judah, when the kings and the people were turning from the Lord. The prophets condemned people's sin – turning from God – and the sins in society that resulted from this: injustice, oppression of the poor, sexual immorality, and greed. They spoke out against pride and hypocrisy, saying that religious externals were of no consequence if people's hearts and actions were far from God.

They declared that God would be faithful to his promises to punish the people if they rebelled against him. The judgment – referred to as the "day of the LORD" – is frightening and inescapable:

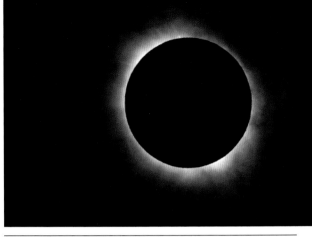

The great day of the LORD is near –
  near and coming quickly.
The cry on the day of the LORD is bitter;
  the Mighty Warrior shouts his battle cry.
That day will be a day of wrath –
  a day of distress and anguish,
    a day of trouble and ruin,
  a day of darkness and gloom,
    a day of clouds and blackness...

Zephaniah 1:14–15

Darkness was a sign of God's judgment

The main judgment in view is that of the exile. Some prophets spoke long before the exile, looking to it as a future event. Others ministered at the time of the exile, explaining why it was happening. Still others lived after the return and indicated that there was still a future day of judgment, of which the destruction of Jerusalem was only a foreshadowing.

Hope

The prophets also spoke of God's grace, and of hope beyond judgment. The prophets develop and expand on the promises already made to Abraham. There would be a new king, a new temple, a new covenant, even a new creation. This hope would only be realized the other side of judgment and exile: it would be a salvation *through* judgment. The nation needed to die to her old way of sin once and for all, and be raised with a new heart and a new spirit. This is how the people could finally have a relationship with God in a new and perfected Eden, as God had always planned.

LOOKING AHEAD TO JESUS:
All promises are "yes" in him

The apostle Paul says that all God's promises are "yes" in Christ (2 Corinthians 1:20). For many prophecies, this means they will not be fulfilled literally (for example in the physical land of Israel) but in a far greater way in Christ's new creation kingdom. One writer gives the example of a boy in the year 1900, promised a horse and cart by his father when he gets married. By the time the boy marries, the car has been invented, and that is what his father gives him as a means of transport. The father has kept his promise – but in a greater way than expected.[9]

God gave his people promises in language they could understand, but the fulfilment often far surpasses what the people of the day might have expected. With any prophecy, it is important to ask how it is ultimately fulfilled in Christ and his kingdom.

ISAIAH: PROPHECY OF A NEW HEAVENS AND EARTH

Isaiah has been called "the Gospel of the Old Testament". It is quoted in the New Testament more than twice as much as any other prophet, and was a key source for the New Testament church to understand the person and work of Jesus. From the "Christmas passages" of "To us a child is born, a son is given" to the suffering servant passages of him who was "pierced for our transgressions and bruised for our iniquities", the book of Isaiah paints a vivid portrait of Jesus and the salvation he brings.

Call of Isaiah

Isaiah's call in chapter 6 is a microcosm of the whole book. Isaiah's experience was a model for what the people of Isaiah's day needed – and indeed all God's people need – in order to be useful for him:

A bigger view of God. For Isaiah, this was seeing a vision of the Lord in the Temple, high and lifted up, with angels crying, "Holy, holy, holy". Isaiah's ministry would be to show the people the glory of this God, and the central section of Isaiah (40–55) is one of the most elevated and majestic presentations of the Lord in all of Scripture.

A clearer view of their sin. Faced with the holiness of God, Isaiah was confronted with the sin of both himself and the people. Much of the book of Isaiah is an indictment of the people's sin, in particular that of *pride*, failing to see themselves properly in relation to God as Isaiah did.

A deeper understanding of forgiveness. God sent an angel to touch Isaiah's lips with a coal from the altar, to take his guilt away. The suffering servant of Isaiah 40–55 shows the Lord's greater condescension: sending a servant who would not just take the people's sin away, but do so by taking it on himself. God's grace is what will turn the people's wayward hearts back to God.

Isaiah's Lips Anointed with Fire by Benjamin West

Behold your God!

One of the key questions in the book of Isaiah is "Who will you trust?" The first part of the book is set in the latter days of the kingdom of Judah, with both Egypt and Assyria as rising powers threatening Judah. Will the people look to human alliances – first with Egypt, then with Babylon – to protect them against the Assyrian threat? Or will they look to their Lord?

Isaiah 40–55 gives what the people need: a vast and elevated view of God. The Lord is proclaimed as the one who holds the waters in his hands; who sits enthroned above all peoples and nations; who makes kings rise and fall; who is the first and last; who always acts for his own glory; who directs all history by his powerful word; who declares the end from the beginning; who is utterly free, and will accomplish all he purposes. No one else is like this God. There is no one else so holy. No one else so righteous. No one else so powerful.

New creation

Isaiah speaks of a glorious future beyond the judgment – a new exodus, this time out of captivity in Babylon. But Isaiah looks beyond even this to a greater future:

"Who has measured the waters in the hollow of his hand, or with the breadth of his hand marked off the heavens?" (Isaiah 40:12)

> *See, I will create a new heavens and a new earth. The former things will not be remembered, nor will they come to mind. But be glad and rejoice forever in what I will create, for I will create Jerusalem to be a delight and its people a joy. I will rejoice over Jerusalem and take delight in my people; the sound of weeping and of crying will be heard in it no more.*
>
> Isaiah 65:17–19

God's creation plans will be fulfilled. Eden will be expanded to the end of the earth and God's redeemed people will rejoice in him forever.

LOOKING AHEAD TO JESUS:
The Servant Songs

Isaiah speaks of the majestic power of God, but also of his humility, seen primarily in the "Servant Songs". God's good purposes will be achieved through a "servant" figure. In Isaiah's day it was not clear who this servant would be, but the New Testament makes it clear this is Jesus.

1st Servant Song: Isaiah 42:1–9	The gentleness of the servant: "A bruised reed he will not break, and a smouldering wick he will not snuff out" (verse 3).
2nd Servant Song: Isaiah 49:1–12	The servant's restoring work will not just be for Israel. God says to him: "I will also make you a light for the Gentiles, that my salvation may reach the ends of the earth" (verse 6).
3rd Servant Song: Isaiah 50:4–9	The servant's speech will be gracious: "The Sovereign LORD has given me a well-instructed tongue, to know the word that sustains the weary" (verse 4).
4th Servant Song: Isaiah 53	The servant will suffer, and his suffering will be for the sins of the people: "He was pierced for our transgressions, he was crushed for our iniquities; the punishment that brought us peace was on him, and by his wounds we are healed" (verse 5).

JEREMIAH: PROPHECY OF A NEW COVENANT

Jeremiah is known as the "weeping prophet", as he laments the state of his nation and how they have turned from the Lord. Though he is just a youth, the Lord touches Jeremiah's lips and puts words in his mouth. Jeremiah's prophetic ministry will be a hard one: "to uproot and tear down, to destroy and overthrow, to build and to plant" (1:10). The harvesters' arms would be full of grain again, but not yet. There is hope of a golden future, but it will only come through the devastation of exile.

Jeremiah, the "weeping prophet" from a fresco by Michaelangelo in the Sistine Chapel

Sin as idolatry

Jeremiah prophesied in the very last days of the kingdom of Judah, and the book concludes with a postscript recording the fulfilment of Jeremiah's prophecies in the destruction of Jerusalem. Much of the book records Jeremiah rebuking the people for their sin, and calling for repentance.

Jeremiah describes sin in relational terms – as *idolatry*. The Lord brought Israel out of Egypt, and at Sinai made them his people – his *bride*. Israel have been unfaithful: they have turned aside to other gods, and as such they are accused of spiritual adultery, and even prostitution (5:7). The sin is all the greater because of the amazing love and care God has shown them, and because of the failure of the other "gods" to provide for them in any way: "My people have committed two sins: They have forsaken me, the spring of living water, and have dug their own cisterns, broken cisterns that cannot hold water" (2:13).

False religion

Despite the prophet's repeated warnings of judgment, the people of Jeremiah's day were complacent and thought that they would be safe. False prophets said to the people, "Peace, peace..." when there was no peace (6:14, 8:11). The people thought that because the Temple was still standing and their religious heritage intact, they would be spared. Jeremiah warned them of the folly of this: "Do not trust in deceptive words and say 'This is the temple of the LORD, the temple of the LORD, the temple of the LORD!'" (7:4). As so often happened in the Old Testament, spiritual sin led to societal sin. The people of Jeremiah's day seemed very religious, yet this was a cover to hide their oppression of immigrants, orphans, and widows.

Would repentance change things?

There is a tension running through the book of Jeremiah. Over 100 times the people are called to "repent" and be saved. Yet the judgment that Jeremiah announces – that of exile from the land – is presented as inevitable. God is willing to forgive his people, but they are unwilling to turn back to him (5:23). What the people need is a new heart (17:9, 24:7).

Asherah was one of the false gods worshipped by Cannanites

Judgment and hope

Judgment will fall. Before the Lord builds up, he will tear down. Judah will drink the cup of God's wrath (25:15), as Jerusalem and the Temple are destroyed by Nebuchadnezzar. God's people will remain in Babylon for seventy years (25:11). The book of Lamentations, thought by some to be written by Jeremiah, is an eyewitness lament of this destruction of Jerusalem, with all the sorrow and heartache that such an event caused.

But beyond judgment there is hope. God says:

My eyes will watch over them for their good, and I will bring them back to this land. I will build them up and not tear them down; I will plant them and not uproot them. I will give them a heart to know me, that I am the LORD. They will be my people and I will be their God, for they will return to me with all their heart.

Jeremiah 24:6–7

New covenant

Central to the hope offered in Jeremiah is the promise of the new covenant, which addresses the main problem expressed in Jeremiah: the people's faithlessness. This is the new covenant Jesus would speak of at the Last Supper, and bring about through his death:

After the judgment of exile, God promised to bring the people back and plant them in the land again

"I will put my law in their minds
  and write it on their hearts.
I will be their God,
  and they will be my people.
No longer will they teach their neighbour,
  or say to one another, 'Know the Lord,'
because they will all know me,
  from the least of them to the greatest,"
declares the Lord.
"For I will forgive their wickedness
  and will remember their sins no more."

Jeremiah 31:33–34

A new heart	God will make obedient faith a possibility. This is the obedient faith that the covenants with Abraham and Moses required, and which the people in Jeremiah failed to have.
A new relationship	Priests and prophets will no longer be necessary: *all* believers will have personal knowledge of God.
A new forgiveness	Though there was forgiveness in the sacrificial system, under the new covenant there would be a full and final dealing with sin.

LOOKING AHEAD TO JESUS:
New exodus

Jeremiah, like Isaiah, prophesied a new exodus, which would be greater even than the exodus from Egypt. There would be a return from Babylon, a new entry into the Promised Land (Jeremiah 16:14–16). Jeremiah speaks of "fishermen" who will catch the people and bring them back – an image Jesus himself would use when he called his disciples to be "fishers of people" (Mark 1:17). The new exodus Jeremiah prophesied would only be partly fulfilled in the return from Babylon. Jesus himself would bring the true new exodus, delivering his people from slavery and bringing them into the Promised Land of his kingdom.

EZEKIEL: PROPHECY OF A NEW TEMPLE

Like Isaiah and Jeremiah, the book of Ezekiel presents a majestic view of God. The book begins with Ezekiel's vision of God's mighty throne-chariot, coming in judgment *against* God's people. Ezekiel sees four fearsome living creatures, wheels within wheels, and a wild thunderstorm. And all of this is just the *appearance* of the *likeness* of the glory of the Lord. The glory of the Lord himself is beyond description. God will make himself known through his actions in history, so that all the people "shall know that I am the LORD" – a phrase that occurs sixty-eight times in the book.

God's glory leaving the Temple

Ezekiel was a priest, one of the first group to be taken into exile in Babylon in 597 BC. As the book of Ezekiel begins, the Temple was still standing, and Jerusalem had not been destroyed (see p. 82). The first part of Ezekiel is a message of judgment on those who remained in Jerusalem. Ezekiel condemned their sin, beginning with the Temple, which had become polluted and pagan. Ezekiel saw a vision of the glory of the Lord leaving the Temple, which was a spiritual disaster (Ezekiel 10). How could the land be the land of promise, the new Garden of Eden, if the Lord did not dwell there? How could Israel call herself God's people if God did not reside in her midst?

The inescapability of judgment

Multiple prophecies of judgment follow, both condemning the people's sin and warning them of the punishment that would follow. This judgment is inevitable and inescapable. The only hope is for salvation *beyond* the judgment of exile. Only after the fall of Jerusalem, recorded in chapter 33, does Ezekiel present his prophecies of hope.

Babylon where Ezekiel lived in exile

New heart and new spirit

God gave Ezekiel a vision of a valley full of dry bones as a picture of the state of God's people. Dead and in the dust, without any life or future. They have no hope of improving their situation, any more than dry bones are able to give themselves life. The people need *resurrection*.

God told Ezekiel to prophesy over the bones, speaking God's word to them. Before Ezekiel's very eyes, the bones came together with a great rattling, and sinews and flesh and skin appeared on them. God told Ezekiel to prophesy again, and breath (the same word for Spirit) entered the dead people; they came to life and stood on their feet, a vast army (37:7–10).

This vision pictured the new life God would show his people through his spirit (see p. 134).

Ezekiel's vision of a valley of dry bones

LOOKING AHEAD TO JESUS:
New David

The people in Ezekiel's day had faithless and immoral leaders who led them astray, so that they were like sheep without a shepherd (34:5). God promised a new David, who would feed them and be their shepherd (34:23). Yet he also promised that he, the Lord, would be their shepherd (34:15). This expresses a tension that has run throughout the history of the monarchy, indeed right back to Adam's rule in the Garden of Eden. God always intended creation to be ruled by a human king, yet it is clear that only God himself is worthy of such a position. This will be resolved in Jesus Christ, son of David and Son of God.

I will give you a new heart and put a new spirit in you; I will remove from you your heart of stone and give you a heart of flesh. And I will put my Spirit in you and move you to follow my decrees and be careful to keep my laws. Then you will live in the land I gave your ancestors; you will be my people, and I will be your God.

Ezekiel 36:26–28

Flowing rivers symbolize life

New temple

The final eight chapters of the book describe a glorious, new temple. This directly answers the problem expressed in Ezekiel: the Lord's presence leaving his people. The temple here is presented, like the old Temple, with Edenic ornamentation (41:18–20), indicating that the prophecy here is of a return to God dwelling with his people as he did in Eden. Significantly, the glory of the Lord fills the temple (just as it had departed the Jerusalem Temple) indicating God's desire to "live among them forever" (43:9).

From the temple a river flows to the East, getting deeper as it flows, with the power to make the saltwater sea fresh and bring life. Trees on either bank of the river bear fruit every month, the fruit used for food and the leaves for healing (47:12). The symbolism is clear: God will dwell amongst his people, and blessing will flow to the world. This image recurs in the last chapter of the Bible: the river of life flowing from the New Jerusalem, with the tree of life on either side, whose leaves are for the healing of the nations (Revelation 22:1–2). This temple will not be an earthly one built by human hands, but will be the new creation itself, the city built by God, where he will dwell with his people.

This glorious temple vision is the climax of the book, and the last words of the book sum up the hopes of this future, glittering city. Those in exile in Babylon, and those facing the destruction of Jerusalem, had a ravishing picture of hope: a different city to look for, whose chief splendour was not all the jewels, nor the riches and finery, but the name the city is given: "The Lord is there" (Ezekiel 48:35).

DANIEL AND ESTHER: LIVING AS EXILES

God's people were in exile. Far from God and far from hope. Could they still sing the Lord's song whilst in a foreign land? This is more than just an historical question; the apostle Peter describes Christian believers as "exiles" and "strangers", and so the lessons from Daniel and Esther of how to live as exiles are just as relevant today (1 Peter 1:17).

The lion at the Ishtar Gate in Babylon

Daniel: The Most High is sovereign

Daniel was a Jew who was taken to Babylon in the very first group of exiles when Nebuchadnezzar first attacked Jerusalem. He was instructed in the ways of the Babylonians and served in the king's court, but refused to defile himself by eating the king's food (chapter 1). Daniel 2–7 are a concentric structure, with the important theological message at the centre: despite all appearances, God is in control.

Ch. 2	Four mighty kingdoms defeated by the kingdom of God.	**Dream of four-part statue.** Nebuchadnezzar dreams of a statue with head of gold, chest of silver, waist of bronze, and feet of iron and clay. These parts represent four successive kingdoms (most likely Babylon, Persia, Greece, and then Rome). A "rock" will break these kingdoms, and grow to fill the whole earth.
Ch. 3	God's people afflicted but protected.	**Fiery furnace.** Shadrach, Meshach, and Abednego refuse to bow down and worship an image that Nebuchadnezzar sets up of himself. They are thrown into the fiery furnace but are unharmed, and a fourth figure is seen with them in the fire, one who looks like "a son of the gods" (3:25).
Ch. 4	A proud ruler brought low.	**Dream of a tree.** Nebuchadnezzar dreams of a mighty tree that is chopped down. This represents him, and he is humbled and becomes like a beast of the field.
	(Theological message at the centre)	"The Most High is sovereign over all kingdoms on earth and gives them to anyone he wishes... His dominion is an eternal dominion; his kingdom endures from generation to generation" (4:32, 34).
Ch. 5	A proud ruler brought low.	**Writing on wall.** A later king, Belshazzar, is having a feast, using the holy vessels from God's Temple to serve the drink. Writing appears on the wall, which is a message of judgment from God. That very night he is killed by the Persian army.
Ch. 6	God's people afflicted but protected.	**Lion's den.** King Darius issued a decree that no one was allowed to pray to anyone but him. Daniel refused to stop praying to the Lord, and was thrown into the lion's den. The Lord shut the lions' mouths, and Daniel emerged the next day unharmed.
Ch. 7	Four mighty kingdoms defeated by the kingdom of God.	**Dream of four beasts.** Daniel has a vision of four terrifying beasts, representing the kings of the kingdoms in ch. 2. Then he sees the Ancient of Days (God the Father) on his throne and one coming to him who is "like a Son of Man", who is given an eternal kingdom.

Daniel in the Lion's Den by Briton Riviere

Chapters 8–12 record further visions of Daniel, which speak of the suffering God's people must face before their ultimate vindication and deliverance. The book ends with a call to wait patiently.

The message of Daniel

Daniel is a model of how to live in exile. He does not withdraw from life – he serves the king, and seeks the good of the city in which he finds himself (compare to Jeremiah 29:7). Yet neither does he compromise – he risks the king's anger, and being left behind in his professional life, because he determines there are some things he will not do (Daniel 1:8). Most importantly, he lives with a sure knowledge that God is in control, which leads him even to directly disobey the king and risk death (Daniel 6). He does not fear men, because he fears the Lord. God's kingdom will triumph over all earthly powers, but until it does, God's people will suffer – and like Daniel they are called to be faithful, even unto death.

Esther: God's hidden hand

Esther was also a Jew in exile, though much later than Daniel. She was taken into the harem of King Xerxes, one of the most powerful rulers ever in world history to this date. She became aware of the plot of Haman, one of the king's advisors, to exterminate the Jews, and, rather than conceal her ethnicity to save her life, she risked her life by approaching the king to plead for the safety of her people. King Xerxes granted Esther's petition and made a proclamation guaranteeing the safety of the Jews throughout the empire, and the enemies of the Jews were destroyed.

Famously, the book of Esther has no single mention of God, yet God is far from absent. The book is a playing-out of the age-old struggle between the offspring of the serpent – here, Haman – and the offspring of the woman, the Jewish people. In particular, there is one offspring of the woman who risks her own life to defeat the offspring of the serpent, and save the rest of the people. God remains in control, even when he is hidden and seems to be absent. This was an important message for the first readers of Esther, and God's people ever since.

Queen Esther by Edwin Long

LOOKING AHEAD TO JESUS:
Mighty yet compassionate ruler

Jesus is the rock of Daniel 2, whose kingdom will expand to fill the whole earth. Jesus' favourite term for himself was "Son of Man", taken from Daniel 7, showing that he was the one who would receive all power and authority from his father.

Christ is seen in Esther by way of contrast. King Xerxes – like many other rulers in history – used his power to exploit and abuse women; in the kingdom of Christ, women will be served and honoured. Nor will God's Messiah put others down to make himself feel more powerful, as Haman did; rather he will willingly give his own life so that others might receive the blessings of the royal palace.

EZRA AND NEHEMIAH: THE RETURN FROM EXILE

In one sense, the return from exile in Babylon was nothing unusual. Kingdoms rise and kingdoms fall. Just as Babylon had conquered Assyria, so Babylon in turn was overrun by the Persians. Cyrus, king of Persia, had a different attitude towards conquered peoples, and so he sent the Jews back to their homeland. Yet for the people of Israel themselves, the spiritual significance of the return was hard to underestimate. More than that, they understood this to be the Lord's hand: "In order to fulfil the word of the LORD spoken by Jeremiah, the LORD moved the heart of Cyrus king of Persia to make a proclamation..." (Ezra 1:1).

First return and rebuilding of the Temple

Ezra 1–6 recounts the return of the first exiles, led by Zerubbabel, in 538 BC. As the Lord had moved to the heart of Cyrus, so now he moved to the hearts of the people to rebuild the Temple even in the face of opposition. The people sang songs of joy when the foundations were laid, but some of the older people wept (Ezra 3:12). This was because the new temple was a shadow of the glory of the old one; most significantly, there is no mention of the Ark of the Covenant being present, nor did the Lord's glory fill this new

The Cyrus cylinder, from the sixth century BC: an account of the reign of King Cyrus, documenting his policy of returning displaced peoples to their homeland, as happened to the Jewish exiles

temple. Fire – symbolizing God's presence – had fallen at the dedication of the tabernacle, and at the completion of the first Temple. Yet here, no fire fell. The next time fire would fall in Scripture would not be on a building, but at Pentecost in the book of Acts: God would no longer dwell amongst his people in a building, but amongst them personally by his spirit. The rebuilt Temple was a sign that God had not abandoned his promise to dwell with his people, but it also pointed towards a greater fulfilment of this promise that was to come.

Rebuilding of walls

Ezra and Nehemiah – the two main characters in these books that bear their names – were both involved in building protective "walls" for the people. The future security of God's people depended not simply on being protected from external enemies, but also from the sin within their own community.

Ezra rebuilt the wall of "Torah" – the law. As a scribe, he taught God's law, to ensure that the people didn't follow the unfaithful ways of their forefathers which had led to exile in the first place. Ezra read the law aloud to the people, recounting the story of God's faithfulness and the people's unfaithfulness (Nehemiah 8). The returned exiles were to understand their identity by situating themselves in the story of history.

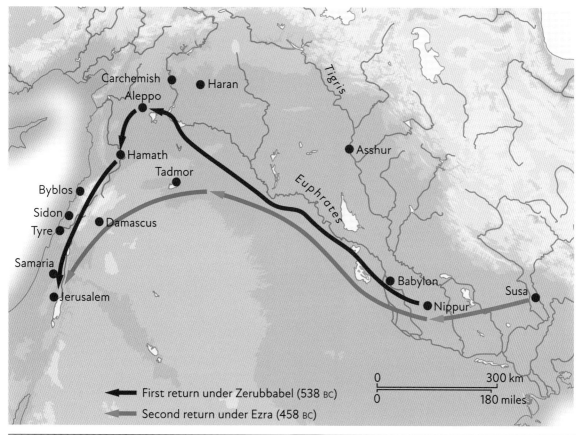

First return under Zerubbabel (538 BC)
Second return under Ezra (458 BC)

The return of exiled Judeans

Nehemiah, whose ministry overlapped with that of Ezra, organized the rebuilding of the walls of Jerusalem. Despite various difficulties, opposition, and plots, the work was finally completed in just fifty-two days (Nehemiah 6:15).

An incomplete return

Ezra and Nehemiah are positive books, yet there are signs that not all is right. In Nehemiah's day the Temple was being neglected – just a few years after it had been rebuilt (Nehemiah 13:11). People showed little concern for God's law, and were intermarrying rather than staying as the pure people of God. Most significantly, this new Temple was not a dwelling place of God among his people.

The people had returned from Babylon, but this was not yet the return they had hoped for, let alone the long-awaited return to Eden. The glorious hopes held out by the prophets had been fulfilled in part, but only in a small part. Nations were not yet streaming to the mountain of the Lord (Isaiah 2:2). No river of blessing was flowing from this Temple to the four corners of the earth (Ezekiel 47). Nor had the people's hearts been changed, or the Spirit been poured out.

Though in the land, in many ways they were still in exile, living the ways of the nations. The spiritual return was not yet complete.

Chronicles: History pointing to the future

The books of Chronicles date from this period. They are a second telling of the history of Israel. The books of Joshua to Kings were written for the people in exile, focusing on the sin of the people and showing that the exile had not been a result of God's powerlessness or faithlessness, but was exactly what he had promised would be the result of unfaithfulness. Chronicles was written for the returned exiles, and gives a more positive retelling of the history, focusing on the priests and the royal line of David. The point was to reassure people of their continuity with the promises of old.

Ezra Reads the Law to the People by Gustave Doré

LOOKING AHEAD TO JESUS:
God has not forgotten his promises

The great return from exile had not been all the people had hoped for, but the books of Chronicles point people to a future hope, because the ancient promises are still intact. A serpent-crusher will come. An offspring of Abraham will bring blessing to the world. A king from David's line will rule in truth and justice. A second Adam will come who will expand the boundaries of God's garden paradise until God's glory covers the earth as the waters cover the sea.

35 MINOR PROPHETS: DARKNESS BEFORE THE DAWN

The "minor prophets" or "Book of the Twelve" were probably written on one single scroll and treated as one book. Some of the Twelve look forward to the coming destruction of the exile. The last three – Haggai, Zechariah, and Malachi – date from after the return from exile. But rather than fitting the minor prophets into the historical narrative, they are intended to be read together as one book – one that tells a story of darkness before the dawn, of judgment then salvation, of death then resurrection. The Twelve are a fitting end to the Old Testament, as the final three books look to the future, showing the story is not yet complete...

Hosea

Hosea presents the story of God and his people as a love story, using the example of Hosea and his unfaithful wife. Though the people have been repeatedly unfaithful and deserve judgment, the message of Hosea is that God is a faithful husband who will not abandon his people.

A plague of locusts symbolized the judgment that would fall on God's people

Joel and Amos

Joel uses the image of a plague of locusts to picture the judgment that will fall on God's people. Amos pictures judgment in terms of famine and drought – the very opposite of the Eden-like fruitfulness God's people were made for.

Obadiah

Obadiah is a brief prophecy of judgment on Edom for their role in Israel's destruction. This is a fulfilment of the promise to Abraham that those who curse his family will be cursed (Genesis 12:3).

Jonah

God tells Jonah to announce judgment on Nineveh, but he refuses and sails off in the opposite direction. A storm arises and Jonah is thrown overboard, only to be swallowed by a fish and after three days vomited out onto dry land. Only then does Jonah go and preach in Nineveh – at which they repent and are saved. The book is a microcosm of Israel's history. Israel was to take God's word to the nations. Like Jonah, Israel did not want other nations to share in the blessings of God, and had to be exiled to the realm of death. Only when "resurrected" on the third day would they be able to complete their mission.

"Though the fig tree does not bud... yet I will rejoice in the LORD." (Habakkuk 3:17-18)

Micah

Micah, like his contemporary Isaiah, prophesied a glorious future, but one that would only come after the fires of judgment had burned. There would be times of great distress, which would only end when a great ruler was born: one who would bring peace to the whole world; one who would be from Bethlehem (Micah 5:2–5).

Nahum

Nahum complements the book of Jonah by announcing judgment on Nineveh, who by this time were oppressing God's people. The Lord will defeat his enemies, and this is good news for God's people who rejoice in his salvation.

Habakkuk

This book is unusual – it comprises questions from the prophet to the Lord. Habakkuk asks "How long, O LORD?", lamenting God's seeming inactivity. His second complaint laments God's mysterious ways: using the Babylonians – the most wicked of all nations – to judge Israel. The third chapter is a psalm, where Habakkuk pledges to keep "living by faith": trusting God for the future, on the basis of his actions in the past.

Zephaniah

Zephaniah describes the coming judgment as "a day of darkness and gloom" (Zeph 1:15). This was fulfilled when Jerusalem was destroyed by the Babylonians, and also points to the final day of judgment when God will judge the whole world. Yet this "darkness and gloom" was what happened when Jesus died on the cross (Mark 15:33). As he died, Jesus was taking the punishment that his people deserved, so that they might be spared from the judgment to come.

Haggai

This book records the Lord's command to rebuild the Temple after the exile. Adam's task of filling the earth with God's glory remains in place. Like the end of Ezekiel, Haggai ultimately points to a greater glory of the new Temple that will only be fully fulfilled in the new creation (Revelation 21 and 22).

Zechariah

Zechariah prophesied at the same time as Haggai, to those who had returned from exile. Yet the book opens with the Lord saying, "Return to me." The return from exile was not the final fulfilment of God's plans – there is a spiritual return that still needs to happen. The people were back in the land, but their hearts were still far from God. Zechariah

Hosanna by Laura James shows Jesus entering Jerusalem on a donkey in fulfilment of Zechariah's prophecy

looks forward to the future peace and prosperity of Zion, one which will be achieved through a humble and gentle king who will ride on a donkey (Zechariah 9:9).

LOOKING AHEAD TO JESUS:
Waiting

And so, as the sun sets on the Old Testament, the story is incomplete. Promises are still unfulfilled. For 400 years God is silent and the people are left waiting. Waiting for a messenger. Waiting for the Lord.

Malachi

The Old Testament closes with Malachi pointing to the future. God still loves his people. There is a greater future to look forward to. But repentance is required, and there is further judgment to come, even after exile. The Lord will come to his Temple to purify it for good, and to deal with sin forever. But before that, God will send a messenger like Elijah, to preach repentance and prepare the way for the Lord (Malachi 3:1; 4:5–6).

JESUS: WHO IS THIS MAN?

After darkness, light. Yet this is no slow dawn, no gentle awakening. It is an explosion – of dazzling and startling brightness. The Jesus who strides across Galilee, pulsating with life, is a far cry from the tame pictures of religious art or the "bloodless abstraction" of historians' reconstructions.[10] He seems simply too extraordinary to be allowed. Well might people ask the question, "Who *is* this man?"

The first page of Matthew's Gospel, after a fifteenth-century illuminated manuscript of a Wycliffe Bible

OLD TESTAMENT FULFILMENT:

There is often a blank page in modern Bibles between the Old Testament and the New Testament. But the opening of Matthew's Gospel ties them together. "This is the genealogy of Jesus the Messiah the son of David, the son of Abraham" (Matthew 1:1). Through Jesus the promises to Abraham will be fulfilled. Jesus is the promised king in the line of David. The New Testament encourages readers to keep asking the question: how are all the patterns, promises, and hopes of the Old Testament fulfilled in Jesus?

Beginning with Mark

Matthew was most likely not the first account of Jesus' life to be written – that was Mark's Gospel. Mark begins in the middle of the action. There is relatively little focus on Jesus' teaching, nor is there any account of Jesus' birth. Jesus bursts onto the scene, fully grown, proclaiming the good news of the kingdom of God. For this reason, we start our overview of Jesus in Mark – as this is how many people of that day would have first encountered Jesus. In the following chapters we will trace through more slowly the different stages of Jesus' life, but here we will try to give a glimpse of the whole from Mark's Gospel, aiming to capture something of the amazement that this astonishing figure provoked.

Authority

In Mark's first breathless chapter, Jesus presumes to call twelve men to leave everything to follow him as his disciples, boldly drives out demons, gently restores Simon Peter's mother-in-law with just a touch, and heals a person suffering from leprosy. People marvel at his authority. The second chapter is no less astonishing, as four men bring their paralysed friend to Jesus, and when they find they cannot get to him because of the crowd, they decide to break in through the roof. Imagine the shock of those in the house – not to mention the owners of the house – as

The shores of the Sea of Galilee, the setting for much of Jesus' early ministry

they saw rubble fall from the ceiling, before the man being lowered down on a mat. Imagine the greater shock when Jesus didn't say, "be healed" but instead said, "your sins are forgiven" (Mark 2:5). Jesus was showing that this man's most urgent need – indeed the most urgent need of the whole human race – was forgiveness. He was also showing that he had that authority to forgive, something that only God could do.

Division

The breakneck story continues, with Jesus eating with tax collectors and sinners, healing on the sabbath – exactly the sort of things that infuriated the religious leaders who cared more about rules than people. Many people followed Jesus, but there were many others who found him offensive, including the religious leaders who began plotting to kill him. There was certainly no neutrality when it came to this astonishing man from Nazareth.

Turning point: Who is this man?

After more miracles, culminating in opening the eyes of a blind man, Jesus asked his disciples the question that would be the turning point in the gospel: "Who do people say I am?" (Mark 8:27).

"Who is this man?" is the question that has been underlying every single event in the gospel so far. Jesus has displayed power and authority that only God can possess, he has showed an extraordinary mix of sternness and compassion, boldness and tenderness, and always at the right time. The arrogant have gone away rebuked, the oppressors have been taken down, but the needy have been cared for, and the vulnerable touched with compassion. Who is this man? The conclusion that Mark has told us from the outset is now grasped by Peter, one of the disciples: "You are the Messiah" (8:29). Jesus is the anointed king promised from the Old Testament, the one on whom all the hopes of the people were set.

Jesus' mission to die

Immediately after his identity as king being revealed, Jesus tells the disciples that he must suffer many things and be put to death, and after three days rise again. The disciples have understood that Jesus is the promised king, but they have not understood what sort of king he will be: that he is also the suffering servant (see p. 86). From this point in the gospel, the cross casts its shadow over everything that happens, as Jesus explains how it is through his *death* – not through military conquest – that he will achieve the victory and salvation the disciples long for him to bring.

As the hour of his crucifixion draws nearer, he weeps in agony in the garden of Gethsemane, showing real dread at the agonies that await. Yet moments later this frail man stands trial with poise and grace. He is mocked, spat on, then led out to be crucified, and yet kingly motifs abound. He has a crown – albeit of thorns. The charge against him reads, "The King of the Jews". And when he died, the Roman centurion watching on said, "Surely this man was the Son of God."

An angel told the women that Jesus had risen

LES SAINTES FEMMES AU TOMBEAU

The ending

Mark ends on something of a cliff-hanger. Jesus had been buried and laid in a tomb. On the third day Mary, Mary Magdalene, and Salome went to the tomb and found the stone rolled away and an angel telling them that Jesus has risen. But Jesus himself is not seen again in the Gospel of Mark, and the book ends with the women running away, scared. This ending leaves the story unfinished, with an implicit question to the readers: what do you make of this? It ultimately points back to Jesus' question that dominates the book: "Who do you say I am?" (Mark 8:29).

FOUR GOSPELS: PORTRAITS OF JESUS

The word "gospel" means "good news". First and foremost, the Christian faith is not a list of rules or rituals, nor is it something to restrict or oppress. It is a story with a happy ending. It is the righting of ancient wrongs. It is the fulfilment of centuries-old hopes and dreams. The good news concerns Jesus Christ, God himself come to earth for our salvation. The four eyewitness accounts of his life are called "Gospels" because they record this good news. They all tell the same story, but with different emphases and perspectives – after all, could any one account fully capture the glory of this man from Nazareth?

A page from an ancient Ethiopian Bible

OLD TESTAMENT FULFILMENT

The New Testament portraits of Jesus are painted with colours drawn straight from the Old Testament. Isaiah 40–66 had promised a time of "good news" when God himself would come to reign, care for his people, bring light to the nations, open the eyes of the blind, release the captives, judge his enemies, raise the dead from their graves, pour out his Holy Spirit, and bring salvation to the whole earth. This is what people might have dared to hope might be happening, as Jesus began his ministry by telling people to believe the "good news". Jesus was bringing the glorious restoration of the reign of God. At the very heart of this "good news" was the servant of God who would suffer and die for the sins of his people (Isaiah 53:5–6).

Good news in a Roman context

The word "gospel" also had a Roman background, where it was used to describe the announcement of the birth of an emperor – for example Caesar Augustus in the Priene Calendar Inscription of 9 BC. At the time of Jesus, Israel was under Roman occupation and rule. So when the early Christians called their message "gospel" they were not merely making a claim about individual salvation, but rather announcing the birth of a new ruler, an announcement with public and political implications.

The emperor Caesar Augustus

Overview of four Gospels

Matthew and John were disciples of Jesus, while Mark seems to have received much of his material from the apostle Peter. Luke is the most explicit in describing his method: researching carefully and putting together an "ordered account" based on eyewitness testimony (Luke 1:1–4). Due to the similarities between Matthew, Mark, and Luke, they are known as the "synoptic" gospels (meaning "seen together"). All the four Gospels were written during the lifetime of eyewitnesses who could have challenged the truthfulness of these accounts, but we're not aware of any such claims.

Key features of the four Gospels

	MATTHEW	MARK	LUKE	JOHN
Date (AD)	Early 60s	Late 50s	Early 60s	55–90
Who is Jesus?	Jesus is the fulfilment of age-old hopes. Shows the *length* of God's love.	Jesus is the suffering servant. Shows the *depth* of God's love.	Jesus is the saviour of the *world*. He cares for those less valued by the society of his day: women, the poor, foreigners, those with disabilities. Shows the *breadth* of God's love.	Jesus as God's eternal Son. Shows the *height* of God's love.
Key verse(s)	"This is the genealogy of Jesus the Messiah the son of David, the son of Abraham" (1:1). Also 28:16–20.	"Jesus went into Galilee, proclaiming the good news of God. 'The time has come,' he said. 'The kingdom of God has come near. Repent and believe the good news!'" (1:14–15). "For even the Son of Man did not come to be served, but to serve, and to give his life as a ransom for many" (10:45).	"The Spirit of the LORD is on me, because he has anointed me to proclaim good news to the poor. He has sent me to proclaim freedom for the prisoners and recovery of sight for the blind, to set the oppressed free, to proclaim the year of the LORD's favour" (4:18–19).	"Jesus performed many other signs in the presence of his disciples, which are not recorded in this book. But these are written that you may believe that Jesus is the Messiah, the Son of God, and that by believing you may have life in his name" (20:30–31).
Synoptics vs John	Focus is on Jesus in Galilee. Short sayings and parables. Teaching about the kingdom of God. More narrative.			Focus is on Jerusalem and the Temple. Long discourses. Teaching about identity of Jesus and eternal life. More theology.

Other distinctives	Five extended sections recording Jesus' teaching. Lots of Old Testament quotations.	Amazement. Fast-paced narrative. Lots of miracles.	The Holy Spirit (see p. 156). Luke is the first part of the story continued in Acts.	Seven signs. Seven "I am" statements. Focus on Jewish feasts.
Good questions to ask as you read	What sort of kingdom is Jesus bringing? How is Jesus fulfilling the Old Testament patterns and prophecy?	Who is Jesus? Why did he come? What does it mean to follow him?	What is the good news? Who is the good news for?	What is the relationship between Jesus and the Father? What is eternal life? What does it mean to believe?

In the early church, the four Gospels became linked to the four creatures of Ezekiel 1 and Revelation 4. Matthew: a human, pointing to Jesus as Israel's teacher; Mark: a lion, pointing to Jesus as mighty king; Luke: an ox, pointing to Jesus as the one who bears the world's burdens; John: an eagle, pointing to the exalted nature of Jesus, Son of God. This illustration comes from the Book of Kells

JESUS' BIRTH: HEAVEN EMBRACED EARTH

The birth of Jesus has become so familiar through Christmas scenes that it can be hard to separate the original events from later traditions, let alone recapture the significance of this momentous moment. The Gospels don't mention Christmas trees, snow, or even whether any animals were present, but the reality is still striking. A baby for whom there was no room, and who was laid in an animal's feeding trough. A star marking his arrival. Shepherds visited by angels. Most significantly, a virgin birth.

Virgin birth: Fully human, fully divine

This is how the birth of Jesus the Messiah came about: His mother Mary was pledged to be married to Joseph, but before they came together, she was found to be pregnant through the Holy Spirit.
Matthew 1:18

In just one sentence Matthew records one of the most astonishing events imaginable. Though Mary was still a virgin, she became pregnant with a child.

The virgin birth points to the heart of who Jesus is: fully human and fully divine. His human mother points to his genuine humanity. The absence of a human father points to this being the miraculous work of God: Jesus is nothing less than God himself come to earth. The word "incarnation" refers to God becoming man, from the Latin "in carne" meaning "in flesh".

An African batik showing the birth of Jesus

In the Gospels, Jesus' full humanity and divinity can be seen.

- **Fully human:** He eats, gets tired and sleeps, cries, bleeds, and eventually dies.
- **Fully divine:** He casts out demons, heals the sick, raises the dead.

Many errors in the Christian church have arisen from denying either the full humanity or the full divinity of Jesus, or by trying to merge the two, resulting in a divine–human hybrid (e.g. the view that Jesus had a human body but a divine soul). The Scriptures rather present Jesus who is fully God *and* fully man – not a puzzle to be solved, but a mystery to be adored.

In the town of David

Although Mary and Joseph lived in Nazareth, they were forced to travel to Bethlehem, Joseph's home town, because of a census that was being conducted across the whole Roman empire. Bethlehem, though a small town, was the town of King David, and Joseph belonged to the royal line of David. David had been promised a son who would reign forever, yet there had been no king from David's line for many years. But at that first Christmas, the angels announced: "Do not be afraid. I bring you good news that will cause great joy for all the people. Today in the town of David a Saviour has been born to you; he is the Messiah, the Lord" (Luke 2:10–11).

The words "Messiah" and "Christ" are equivalent words, both meaning "anointed king". "Christ" is not Jesus' surname; it is a kingly title.

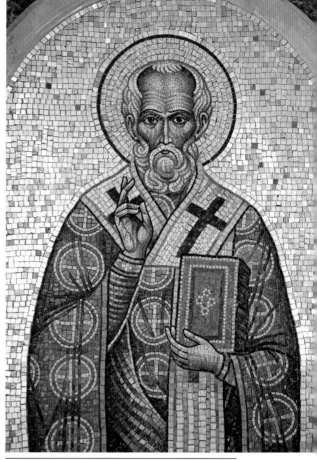

St Nicholas defended the full divinity of Christ

OLD TESTAMENT FULFILMENT

Jesus was born in direct fulfilment of prophecies from hundreds of years before. Micah had promised the great ruler would be born in the small town of Bethlehem (Micah 5:2). Isaiah had promised not just that there would be a virgin birth, but that the one born would be "Immanuel" – God with us (Isaiah 7:14).

The slaughter of the newborns

Herod understood something of the significance of the birth of Jesus. Herod was king of Israel, but he was not from the line of David, and was only in power because the occupying Roman forces had put him there. Herod asked the wise men to let him know once they had found the one born as "king of the Jews." Herod claimed he wanted to worship Jesus, but in fact wanted to kill him. When the wise men were warned by an angel not to go back to Herod, Herod made a decree that all the male children in the region under the age of two years old were to be killed, forcing Jesus and his family to flee to Egypt (Matthew 2:13). Herod, like Pharaoh had been so many years before (p. 32), is a serpent figure, desiring to kill the "offspring of the woman" and oppose the promises of God.

Why did God become man?

For all the questions about *how* God became a man, the most important question is *why*? The answer is found in two names given to Jesus:

Jesus – "The Lord saves" (Matthew 1:21)	**Salvation:** Matthew adds an extra element to "The Lord saves"; in fact, "he will save his people *from their sins*" (1:21, emphasis added). The Jewish people were expecting a military deliverer, but the salvation Jesus came to bring would be much deeper than that. The Old Testament made it clear that God's people needed their sins dealt with. Again and again, the storyline of the Bible seems to have faltered because of human sin – only a definitive dealing with sin would enable all God's promises to come to pass.
Immanuel – "God with us" (Matthew 1:23)	**Revelation.** The key covenant promise God made to his people in the Old Testament is that he would be their God; this comes to fulfilment in Jesus Christ, as God himself came to earth to be with his people. An infinite, invisible God could only be known if he chose to reveal himself to his people. This happened supremely in the person of Jesus Christ: "No one has ever seen God, but the one and only Son, who is himself God... has made him known" (John 1:18).

God didn't simply send a message from heaven saying, "I care." Rather he stepped into the world and touched the man suffering from leprosy, ate with the outcasts. He didn't simply say, "This is how to live." In his life he embodied perfect justice, purity, and generosity. In the Gospels we find the answer to the question, "What would God be like if we saw him face to face?"

Christ was born in Israel, but his coming was for all peoples from all cultures. This mural is from The House of Living God church in Cuba, New Mexico

JESUS' EARLY MINISTRY: THE COMING OF THE LORD

In the face of national decline, increasing sinfulness, and enemy oppression, Isaiah had looked forward to a future hope: the arrival of the Lord God himself to restore his people (Isaiah 52:7–10). Malachi had also promised a day when the Lord would come to his Temple, to purify and to judge, but before that day, Elijah would come (Malachi 3:1). For those who had eyes to see, there *was* an Elijah figure on the scene before Jesus. John the Baptist, wearing a camel's hair cloak like Elijah before him, eating an Elijah-like diet of locusts and wild honey...

Modern-day baptisms in the River Jordan

John the Baptist

John was the last prophet, with a message of coming judgment and the call to repentance. He baptized people in the Jordan river as a symbolic washing away of their sins (Matthew 3:6). The location of the Jordan is significant: this was where the people had entered the Promised Land. John was saying to the people that they effectively needed to enter the land again. They needed a new exodus through water, a new return from exile, a new entry into the kingdom of God. John said that the one who followed him would baptize with the Holy Spirit, washing people from the inside: the defining mark of entry into the kingdom of God.

OLD TESTAMENT FULFILMENT

Although the people had returned from exile (see p. 96), their hearts were still far from God. Jesus came to bring the true return from exile, and to bring all the blessings the prophets had promised would accompany this return. In particular, the promise that God would dwell amongst his people once more.

Jesus' baptism

Jesus came to be baptized by John, not because he himself was sinful, but as a way of identifying himself with the people (Matthew 3:13). As he came up out of the water, the heavens were torn open and the Holy Spirit descended on him like a dove. Isaiah's final prayer had been that God would "tear open the heavens" and come to put all things right (Isaiah 64:1, NRSV), and here this prayer was being answered in Jesus.

A voice came from heaven identifying Jesus as God's "Son" – a reference to the king of Psalm 2 and 2 Samuel 7 – and the one with whom God is "well pleased" – a reference to the suffering servant of Isaiah 42:1.

A ceiling mosaic depicting the baptism of Christ (Arian Baptistery, Ravenna, Italy)

This is the beginning of Jesus' ministry. He is the "Lord" the prophets looked forward to. He will bring the new exodus through the waters of judgment into the Promised Land. Like the kings of the Old Testament, he will be empowered by God's spirit for his kingly role. But the way he will exercise this kingship is not as everyone expected. He will do so as the suffering servant from Isaiah, the one who would be "pierced for our transgressions" (Isaiah 53:5).

Jesus' temptation

Right after Jesus' baptism he was driven out into the wilderness, where Satan tempted him for forty days and nights (Matthew 4:1–11). This was a replaying of Israel's forty years of testing in the desert (see p. 45).

First, Satan tempted Jesus to turn stones into bread, rather than relying on his Father's provision. Second, Satan tempted Jesus to test God by throwing himself down from the Temple, knowing that God's angels would rescue him. Finally, Satan offered Jesus all the kingdoms of the world if he would worship him. Each time Jesus refused Satan, and answered by quoting from Deuteronomy, words taken from Israel's own wilderness testing. Where Israel failed, Jesus succeeded. Jesus' obedience is vital for his saving work: Jesus did not simply come to wash away his people's sin, he also came to live the perfect life that they could not live.

Temptation of Christ (mosaic in Basilica di San Marco, Venice)

OLD TESTAMENT FULFILMENT

Jesus' temptation echoes that of Israel in the wilderness, but also of Adam. Adam's failure in the garden meant humanity was exiled into the wilderness. Jesus' faithfulness in the wilderness meant humanity could be brought back to the garden.

Tempted yet without sin

In the book of Hebrews, Jesus is described as "one who has been tempted in every way, just as we are – yet he did not sin" (Hebrews 4:15). Jesus' temptation was a *real* temptation. He really had to depend on his Father, he really did have to persevere in costly obedience – forty days and nights in the wilderness without food would have left him on the point of starvation. This would not have been easy for him – nor would his entire life of costly obedience to his Father, culminating in his brutal and painful death.

Yet in all this he did not sin. If he had sinned in any way – no matter how small – he would have not been qualified to pay for the sins of his people, nor would he have a life of perfect righteousness to give them. It was only because Jesus was fully man and fully God that he could be the saviour his people need. Only one both fully human and fully divine could be so really tempted, yet so perfectly obedient.

The fact that Jesus was tempted in every way is also a source of comfort to Christians. He is a merciful high priest, able to sympathize with human weaknesses, who knows his people's struggles (Hebrews 4:15).

JESUS' TEACHING: GOSPEL AND KINGDOM

At the heart of Jesus' message was love. Not primarily a message that we should all love each other more – which would be true, but hardly unique. Jesus' message centred on God's love for the world. Jesus did call his people to radical holiness, he did demand costly love for God and for neighbour, but it all begins with *God's* love. The message of Christianity is not so much "Here are the things we must *do*," but "Here is what God has *done*."

John 3:16 – Eternal life

> *God so loved the world that he gave his one and only Son, that whoever believes in him shall not perish but have eternal life.*
>
> John 3:16

The good news has its origin in God himself, who *is* love. Without God's love all humanity would perish. All people have turned away from God and are under the same sentence of condemnation as Adam. Sin has been the problem right from the start. Throughout the Old Testament no true resolution has been found. The solution is God giving his only Son, Jesus, to die in the place of his people, to take their condemnation, so that instead they might enjoy life with God. This is the message that is called the "good news" or "gospel".

When he met a paralysed man, Jesus showed his priorities by *first* dealing with the man's greatest problem – sin – before healing him also. A mosaic from Ravenna

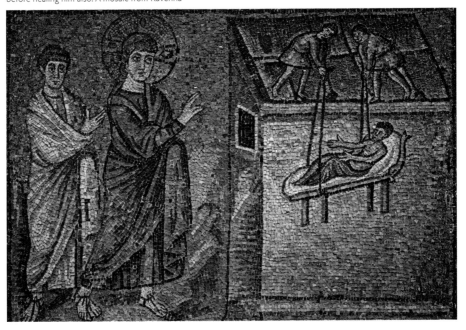

Repentance and faith

The gospel calls for the response of repentance and faith (Mark 1:15). These two are so closely bound together that even when only one word is used – for example John focuses on faith – both concepts are implied.

Repentance. The Old Testament background for the word "repent" is that of turning around. It speaks of a change of direction. Repentance is turning away from following other gods, turning away from living for self, turning away from the sins that displease God, and turning to God instead. It is the acknowledgment that Jesus Christ is Lord and the desire to live for him.

Belief/faith. Faith is an often-misunderstood concept. It is more than mere mental assent; it involves trust. Because of this, it must always

The Gospel of Matthew proclaims Jesus as the new king. This page comes from an Ethiopian school gospel

have an object – be faith *in* something. When someone abseils down a skyscraper, it is not because of a general trust or a warm feeling of "faith". They do it because they believe that the rope will bear their weight. They trust the safety equipment. Christian faith is belief in Jesus Christ. It is trust in his promise to save his people from their sins.

The kingdom of God

Matthew, Mark, and Luke are dominated by references to the "kingdom of God", for example "The time is fulfilled, and the kingdom of God is at hand; repent and believe in the gospel" (Mark 1:15, ESV).

The kingdom of God refers not to God's general rule over all things, but to his particular *saving rule* which has not always been acknowledged on earth. Jesus says the kingdom is now at hand because *he* has come. He is the king of God's kingdom. He is the new David whose rule brings peace and prosperity.

Though the language is different, this is the same message as the message of eternal life in John 3:16. To be part of God's kingdom is to know life and blessing; to be outside of God's kingdom is to perish. The good news of eternal life *is* the good news of the kingdom. The kingdom has come because Jesus is the king. The required response is to repent and believe in him.

Jesus is the true Son of David promised in 2 Samuel 7, the king whose kingdom will never end. For centuries, God's people had languished without a king, and looked back to the glory days of Solomon (see p. 66) who brought peace, joy, and blessing. For Jesus to announce that he was bringing God's kingdom would have filled the hearts of his hearers with hope and expectation that joy might be theirs again.

Present or future kingdom?

The Old Testament expectations were of all of God's promises being fulfilled simultaneously, on the "day of the LORD" (Joel 2:1). Yet the New Testament picture is different. The kingdom does not come all at once – it begins with the first coming of Jesus, but awaits his return to be fully experienced. Many of the parables Jesus told were about the timing, the growth, and the hidden nature of the kingdom. It is like the mustard seed, starting out very small, until it one day becomes the largest tree. It is like the growing seed, which slowly grows both night and day, until the time of harvest.

There is a present *and* a future aspect to the kingdom. Christians therefore speak of living in the "overlap of the ages" – also known in Scripture as the "last days" (see pp. 134–35).

Jesus portrayed as king from the Book of Kells

Parables

Jesus often taught in parables, which were images, short stories, and scenes from daily life. To those who approached the parables genuinely seeking to understand, they made the truths of the kingdom vivid and real. But to those who were sceptical of Jesus, the parables were impossible to understand. The parables were *divisive*.

The parables reflected the kingdom they were used to illustrate. Jesus' kingdom was accessible to all who would come to him humbly, just as the parables were. But to those who came with hard and proud hearts, the door to Jesus' kingdom – and the door to the meaning of the parables – was firmly closed (Mark 4:10–12).

JESUS' MIRACLES: SIGNS OF A RESTORED WORLD

The prophets spoke of a day when the mountains would drip with wine, when the lame would leap for joy, and the blind would see. Jesus' miracles point not simply to his power and divinity, but to the fact that he is the one who will bring these Old Testament promises to pass. His miracles picture the sort of kingdom he is bringing: a world that is entirely restored.

Water into wine

The first miracle in John's Gospel is Jesus turning water into wine. He was at a wedding when the wine ran out and he turned the water from the large stone water jars into fine wine – and large amounts of it (John 2:1–11). Even without the Old Testament background, this would point to Jesus as the source of life and joy. But there is more. Isaiah looked forward to a day when death would be defeated forever, and the people would feast at a wedding banquet on the mountain of God, and drink the finest of wines (Isaiah 25:6–8). These promises are beginning to be fulfilled in Jesus.

One of Jesus' first miracles was turning water into wine at the wedding feast

Even the wind and waves obey him

On one occasion, Jesus and his disciples were in a boat on Lake Galilee when a furious wind arose threatening to drown them all. Jesus, who had been sleeping, rebuked the wind with a word and it died down. On another occasion, he walked on the water, and even enabled Peter to do so with him. In the Old Testament, only God had such power over creation. But also, the sea symbolized all that was evil and threatening to God's people. In showing his power to calm even the fiercest storm, and to tread down the waves, Jesus showed that he had come to conquer evil and push back the darkness. He is someone who can be trusted when the storms and chaos of life press in.

Jesus Calms the Storm by Laura James

Casting out demons, healing the sick

On many occasions, Jesus encountered people who were possessed by demons. When Jesus cast demons out of people the transformation was immediate. One man had lived naked among the tombs with no one able to approach him. After Jesus healed him he was found clothed and in his right mind, telling everyone how the Lord had been good to him (Mark 5:20). Jesus had come to defeat Satan and to rescue people from his oppressive power.

Jesus also healed many people. In every instance, he was pointing to himself as the one to bring the new creation, the days heralded by Isaiah when the blind would see, the lame walk, and the prisoners be freed. But it is striking to see *how* Jesus healed. When confronting demons he was loud and commanding, showing his authority. But when healing Simon Peter's mother-in-law just a while later, he didn't speak at all; he just gently took her by the hand. Moments after great power, he showed great tenderness (Mark 1:21–31). He was gently restoring the brokenness that had come into the world through the fall. When God came to earth, he was not found in royal palaces, but at the bedside of the sick.

OLD TESTAMENT FULFILMENT

Seven hundred years before Jesus, Isaiah promised a coming time of the Lord's salvation: "Then will the eyes of the blind be opened and the ears of the deaf unstopped. Then will the lame leap like a deer, and the mute tongue shout for joy" (Isaiah 35:5–6). Jesus' miracles are signs that these promises are being fulfilled in him.

Moved with compassion

Jesus' compassion is highlighted when he healed a man with leprosy. This man would have been forced to live away from society for fear of passing on the disease. More than that, he would have been a spiritual outcast, seen as "unclean" and unable to enter the Temple or the presence of God. Perhaps he had gone his entire adult life not knowing the touch of another human.

Mark records Jesus being "moved with compassion" when he saw the man (1:41, KJV). Where others moved away from this man, Jesus did what he always did to those in need – he moved toward him. He even touched him. Jesus was able to heal "at a distance" – he didn't *need* to touch the man. But he chose to. Many people view God as distant or cold or uninterested. They see themselves as too far gone, too dirty to merit the attention of this deity. How different to this man's experience. In the compassionate face of Jesus, he saw the face of a God who cared.

Power over death

Three times in the Gospels Jesus raised someone from the dead, perhaps the most poignant being his friend Lazarus. Mary and Martha had sent for Jesus because their brother Lazarus was ill. But Jesus stayed two more days where he was before coming, and when he arrived, Lazarus had already died. Jesus used these events to demonstrate something vital about his identity and work: "I am the resurrection and the life. The one who believes in me will live, even though they die; and whoever lives by believing in me will never die" (John 11:25–26). Jesus had come to break the power of death. His raising of Lazarus from the grave would be a pointer to what Jesus would one day do for all his people.

In this scene, we see Jesus at his most powerful *and* most tender. As he is taken to the grave of Lazarus, and sees the place where he was laid, "Jesus wept" (John 11:35). Even though Jesus knew he was about to raise Lazarus, he still felt the pain of loss. Death and sorrow moved him deeply, and they move him still.

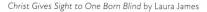

Christ Gives Sight to One Born Blind by Laura James

DISCIPLES AND OPPONENTS: JESUS' IDENTITY

Jesus was a divisive figure. He was adored and cherished by many who followed him, yet others – in particular the powerful leaders – felt threatened by him and opposed him. Very few people were left indifferent – his claims were far too vast for that to be possible. How people responded to him depended on the question of his *identity*.

Walk in the Park by Laila Shawa. Many women followed Jesus, including Mary Magdalene, Joanna, and Susanna, who were among his closest friends and supported him out of their own resources

Who is Jesus?

The turning point in the synoptic gospels occurs when Jesus asks his disciples who people say he is. Various options are given: John the Baptist, Elijah, or one of the prophets. Though these are all very elevated titles, they are insufficient. Then Jesus asks his disciples who they think he is. Peter responds, "You are the Messiah" – the long-awaited king from David's line (Matthew 16:16; Mark 8:29; Luke 9:20).

The sort of king the people were expecting was a military king who would come and immediately defeat the Romans. But Jesus' kingship was to be altogether different. Straight after being acknowledged as the Messiah, Jesus told his disciples that he must be betrayed, suffer, and die, then on the third day rise again. Jesus' kingship could only be understood in light of the cross.

Cross-shaped discipleship

After teaching about his own death and resurrection, Jesus immediately called for his disciples also to "take up their cross" and follow him (Mark 8:34). The pattern is clear. Christian discipleship is always cross-shaped. It is the surrendering of one's life and privileges now for the sake of following Jesus. But just as Jesus died but then rose, so his followers who lay their lives down for his sake will receive resurrection life together with him. Disciples are not those who are perfect, or never stumble. Jesus' first disciples failed on many occasions. But the way of discipleship was the same as the way of becoming a believer in the first place: repentance and faith (see p. 115). Daily turning away from sins to God, daily depending on his all-sufficient forgiveness.

The twelve apostles

Jesus had many disciples (which means "followers"), but he chose twelve to be "apostles", with special authority to be witnesses of all he said and did, and to pass that message on (Mark 3:13–19). The New Testament books were all written by an apostle or closely based on an apostle's teaching.

Jesus chose *twelve* apostles, matching the twelve tribes of the Old Testament. Jesus was making the point that membership of God's people would no longer be based on descent from Abraham, but on relationship with *him*.

Kingdom living

Jesus taught that no one by their good deeds could earn anything from God. Salvation was entirely on the basis of what God had done, to be received by faith.

Yet to those who would follow him, Jesus called for a radical holiness. In his Sermon on the Mount (Matthew 5–7), he called his followers to a holiness that was not merely external (e.g. "Do not murder") but also internal: "Do not be angry with your brother" (Matthew 5:21–22). He condemned pride, and encouraged humility. Good deeds were to be done for the approval of God, not for the approval of other humans.

The standing figures of the twelve apostles from an Ethiopian Bible

Jesus didn't just call for holiness, he made it *possible*. Through Christ, Christians know God as Father – a dominant emphasis in the Sermon on the Mount. Knowledge of God as Father is what enables Christians to surrender their rights, put others first, forgive from the heart, trust God even in hardship, and seek first God's kingdom and his righteousness.

Jesus' opponents

Jesus encountered opposition from the very early days of his ministry. When he told the paralyzed man that his sins were forgiven, the religious leaders accused Jesus of blasphemy, as only God could forgive sins (Mark 2:7). When Jesus healed on the sabbath, the religious leaders hated it, because they recognized that Jesus was acting with God's authority, making himself equal with God (John 5:17).

Jesus was also opposed because of what he said about the identity of his hearers. He said that all people – whether "moral" and respectable or not – were spiritually sick and needing a doctor (Mark 2:17). Those who admitted their sin found acceptance and compassion from Jesus. But those who claimed moral superiority found his message offensive.

Many today say they like the teaching of Jesus, even if they don't follow him. But in Jesus' day no one responded like this. It was Jesus' teaching that got him into trouble. He claimed to be God. People either believed this and followed him, or wanted to kill him.

JESUS' FINAL DAYS: MINISTRY IN JERUSALEM

Passover was a joyous annual celebration when the Jewish people celebrated their deliverance from Egypt centuries earlier. Jerusalem would have swelled to many times its normal population with thousands and thousands of pilgrims coming from across the land to celebrate the feast. It was a time of nationalistic fervour, a time that made the occupying Roman forces very uneasy. Imagine their concern when Jesus arrived, surrounded by crowds and deliberately fulfilling kingly prophecies from the Old Testament...

Before going to Jerusalem, Jesus went up a high mountain with Peter, James, and John, and he was "transfigured". This fifteenth-century mural is in the church of the Saviour, Paleochorio, Cyprus

The transfiguration

Just before going to Jerusalem, Jesus went up a high mountain with Peter, James, and John, and he was "transfigured" before them. His face shone like the sun and his clothes were as white as light. Moses and Elijah appeared with him, and spoke to him, then a bright cloud overshadowed them and a voice came from heaven saying, "This is my Son, whom I love; with him I am well pleased. Listen to him!" (Matthew 17:5). The disciples with Jesus fell face-down, terrified, and when they dared look up they saw only Jesus; Moses and Elijah had gone.

It would be hard to overstate the majesty of this scene. The disciples saw God face-to-face in his glory. Perhaps before the darkness of the cross, the disciples needed a glimpse of the undimmed brightness of Jesus' glory. They needed to know the one who would hang in agony was the same one who hung the heavens in place. The one who would cry, "It is finished," was the same one who had been there at the beginning. The one who would bow his head in shadow was the same one who had said, "Let there be light."

Artwork on the door of the Holy Sacrament Church, Dasso, Benin, showing Jesus entering Jerusalem on Palm Sunday

OLD TESTAMENT FULFILMENT

The words God spoke to Jesus from heaven – very similar to those at his baptism – are all drawn from the Old Testament. "My son" – showing Jesus to be the king of Psalm 2; "Whom I love" – showing Jesus to be the suffering servant of Isaiah 42:1; "Listen to him" – showing Jesus to be the true and final prophet of Deuteronomy 18.

The triumphal entry

Jesus entered Jerusalem on a donkey, and the crowds – most likely those from Galilee who knew him and were also coming to Jerusalem for Passover – spread their cloaks on the ground and waved palm branches. This "triumphal entry" is soaked in Old Testament allusions. The crowds sing words taken from Psalm 118 – a psalm celebrating the great deliverance of God's people – "Hosanna to the Son of David! Blessed is he who comes in the name of the Lord!" (Matthew 21:9). Jesus rides a donkey to fulfil the prophecy of Zechariah: "Rejoice greatly, Daughter Zion! Shout, Daughter Jerusalem! See, your king comes to you, righteous and victorious, lowly and riding on a donkey, on a colt, the foal of a donkey" (Zechariah 9:9).

Cleansing of the Temple

Jesus came into the Temple, and saw that it had become a den of robbers, rather than a house of prayer for all nations. Jesus overturned the tables of the money-changers and drove out those selling animals. This was real anger, and zeal for the honour of the Lord (Mark 11:15–19). The Old Testament had ended with Malachi promising a day when the Lord would come to his Temple: a great "day of the LORD" judgment when the Lord would come with fire, when no root and branch of wickedness would remain (Malachi 4:1). This is the context in which Jesus' cleansing of the Temple must be understood.

The destruction of the Temple

On another occasion, the disciples pointed out to Jesus the magnificence of the Temple. Jesus' response was stark: "Truly I tell you, not one stone here will be left on another; every one will be thrown down" (Matthew 24:2). Jesus then spoke of the destruction of the Temple – words that were fulfilled when the Romans destroyed Jerusalem around forty years later in AD 70. As when the Temple had been destroyed in Old Testament days, it is hard to imagine a more unsettling event to happen for the Jewish people. To lose the Temple was to lose what made the land and the people distinctive: God's dwelling in their midst.

The destruction of the Temple would be the final falling of the covenant curses for the people's disobedience, from Deuteronomy. No longer would this building be the place where God met with his people. Jesus had come as the true Temple – the true meeting place of God and man. He had come to make access to God available to all who trusted in him.

Betrayal and devotion

While Jesus was in Jerusalem, the chief priests and elders got together to plot to arrest Jesus and kill him. They were scared of making a public arrest, because it might cause a riot during the Passover celebrations. Judas Iscariot, one of Jesus' disciples, agreed to deliver Jesus over to them at an opportune time, in exchange for thirty pieces of silver (Matthew 26:14–15).

This story is set right next to the story of Jesus eating at the house of Simon the Leper. A sinful woman came to him and poured a very expensive jar of perfume – most likely a family inheritance – over his head. The disciples were indignant, as the perfume was worth a year's wages and could have been used for the poor. But Jesus delighted in this act of devotion: "Why are you bothering this woman? She has done a beautiful thing to me" (Matthew 26:10).

Contrasts abound in these stories. Judas haunts the corridors of power, looking to gain money and influence, and willing to betray his friend in the process. Jesus is found – as he so often was – with the lowest and the least. He gave honour and dignity to those whom most people would have shunned. This sinful woman – probably a prostitute – is someone Jesus is prepared to publicly honour, and someone whose actions he calls beautiful. She, not the religious elite or even the disciples themselves, becomes a model of faith and devotion, someone whose story would be told for millennia to come.

Perfume from bottles such as these was poured over Jesus' head

THE LAST SUPPER: PREPARING FOR THE END

"Do not let your hearts be troubled" (John 14:1). With these tender words, Jesus spoke to his fearful disciples, reassuring them that all that was about to happen was part of his plan. They didn't yet know that the Passover meal they were sharing would later come to be known as "The Last Supper", but they were unsettled by all of Jesus' talks about his imminent departure. Surely this would be a disaster – they had left everything to follow him. Yet Jesus explained to them that his death would not be a failure, but would be the means by which he would fulfil the hopes and prophecies of centuries before them.

The week of Jesus' death

Sunday	Monday	Tuesday	Wednesday	Thursday	Friday	Saturday (sabbath)	Sunday
Entry into Jerusalem.	Cleansing of the Temple.	Teaching in the Temple.	Sanhedrin plot to kill Jesus.	Last Supper. Gethsemane. Arrest of Jesus. Trials begin and proceed through the night.	Trials of Jesus conclude. Crucifixion. Quick burial before the sabbath.	Jesus in tomb.	Women discover empty tomb. Resurrection appearances.

Washing the disciples' feet

Jesus had his disciples prepare an upper room in Jerusalem where they could eat the Passover meal together. Before the meal, Jesus stripped off his outer garment and washed his disciples' feet (John 13:1–20). This was a job so degrading that it was usually reserved only for non-Jewish slaves. Jesus was demonstrating his astonishing love for his disciples and also giving a picture of the greater cleansing he would achieve for them at cross.

A sixth-century mosaic map of Jerusalem

Jesus and the disciples would have been reclining against one another, eating from the same communal dish. It is a very intimate scene. This makes what Jesus says next all the more shocking: he would be betrayed by "one who has dipped his hand into the bowl with me" (Matthew 26:23).

Bread and wine

The different parts of the Passover meal were symbolic, looking back to the Israelites' slavery in Egypt and redemption by the Lord. But Jesus radically redefined Passover. He said it was all about *him*. He took bread and said it was a symbol of his body given for his disciples. He took the cup of wine as a symbol of the new covenant made through his blood. And he told his disciples to share bread and wine regularly in remembrance of him (1 Corinthians 11:23–26). This is the meal that Christians still celebrate today, known as the "Lord's supper", "Communion", or the "Eucharist".

The Last Supper by Simon Ushakov

OLD TESTAMENT FULFILMENT

Jesus was the true and greater Passover lamb, dying in the place of his people, so that they might escape God's judgment. His death would begin a *new* exodus – not out of slavery in Egypt, but out of the greater slavery to sin and death.

Going deeper: The new covenant

By his death, Jesus was initiating the new covenant – the new relationship between God and his people – as promised by Jeremiah and the prophets (see p. 87). But what is "new" about the new covenant? There is much continuity between the new and old covenant (the covenant with Moses). Both are gracious covenants, centring on God's forgiveness, to be received by *faith*. Both have the requirement that faith be expressed in obedient living.

But the new covenant not only replaces but dwarfs the old covenant. The blessings offered are so much greater: life in the new creation kingdom of God, personal knowledge of God for all believers. The forgiveness offered is so much more comprehensive. Forgiveness was available under the old covenant, but "on credit". Jesus' death was the once-for-all sacrifice to fully pay for all his people's sins: past, present, and future.

More than this, the new covenant comes with *power*. The problem with the old covenant with Moses was *not* that it was a covenant based on merit. The problem was that people's hearts were hard, and so they *broke* it. The new covenant comes with a promise of a new heart, of the Spirit poured out, so that God's people *could* respond in faith, and so enjoy the blessings offered them by Christ. The old covenant was a gracious covenant, but in the new covenant God's people knew grace upon grace.

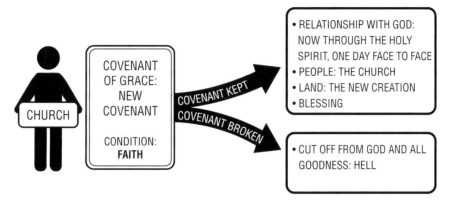

Gethsemane

After supper, Jesus led his disciples just outside Jerusalem to a garden at the foot of the Mount of Olives, called Gethsemane. He told them to wait whilst he went off and prayed. Nowhere in Scripture is the humanity of Jesus more clearly seen, or his emotional life so clearly portrayed: "My soul is overwhelmed with sorrow to the point of death" (Matthew 26:38).

Never has Jesus looked more frail and vulnerable. He longs for any escape from the pain and suffering he is about to go through. Three times he asks his Father if there is any other way. Yet three times he also prays, "Yet not my will, but yours be done" (Luke 22:42). Meanwhile, the disciples have fallen asleep. At the hour when their friend needed them most, they have failed him. Jesus is alone.

Jesus' arrest

Perhaps the sleepy disciples felt a sense of rising dread as they saw torches on the hillside below them. Out of the gloom there appeared a crowd of the religious leaders and armed soldiers, led by Judas. Jesus, however, knew exactly what was happening: "Here comes my betrayer!" (Matthew 26:45).

The Garden of Gethsemane today

Because this arrest took place in the dark, Judas had arranged a signal, to make sure that the chief priests arrested the right man. In one of the most iconic scenes in all of world literature, Judas came up to Jesus and kissed him. Immediately the soldiers laid hands on Jesus and seized him.

Peter – always the most impulsive of the disciples – grabbed a sword and cut off the ear of the high priest's servant. He was prepared to fight for his friend. But Jesus told him to put his sword away. This was all according to plan: "Do you think I cannot call on my Father, and he will at once put at my disposal more than twelve legions of angels? But how then would the Scriptures be fulfilled that say it must happen in this way?" (Matthew 26:53–54).

THE CROSS: THE CENTRE OF THE BIBLE'S STORY

The cross is one of the most well-known symbols in the world today. Crosses adorn buildings and many people wear them around the neck as jewellery. Perhaps they have become so familiar that the significance is lost. The cross was a barbaric form of execution. As the symbol of a religion it was just as shocking as a hangman's noose or electric chair would be today. It was a scandal and stumbling block to many. But according to Jesus, the cross was at the very heart of his mission.

The cross is central to Christianity, and is one of the most well-known symbols in the world today

Why did Jesus die?

Jesus' trials were a sham: conducted at night, with false witnesses, and Jesus given no chance to make a defence. The Jewish council had already decided they wanted him dead, but they didn't have to power to give the death penalty, so they handed him over to the Romans, who did (John 18:30–31). Pilate, the Roman governor, found no guilt in Jesus, but Jerusalem was a tinder-box of nationalistic fervour. And so, fearing a riot or revolution, he gave in to the crowd's demands and delivered Jesus to be crucified.

The crucifixion of Jesus was a wicked act, carried out by wicked men. But it was also part of the good plan of God. Jesus had repeatedly told the disciples that he had to die, that he had come "not to be served but to serve, and to give his life as a ransom for many" (Mark 10:45).

OLD TESTAMENT FULFILMENT

Jesus died willingly, as the full and final sacrifice for sin. All the Old Testament sacrifices – where an animal died in the place of the offerer – were pictures pointing forwards to Christ's death. He died to take the punishment for the sins of his people. Those who trust in Jesus have all their sins paid for in full – there are no more sacrifices that need to be made. This is why Jesus cried, "It is finished" when he died (John 19:30).

The crucifixion

Jesus was scourged (beaten repeatedly with a whip embedded with bone and metal to pierce the flesh), then a crown of thorns was pressed onto his head. He was led out of the city to be crucified.

Crucifixion was a gruesome form of execution, so brutal that the Romans would only use it on foreigners, not their own citizens. The one being crucified was nailed to a cross and left to hang for hours in agony until the life drained out of them.

Jesus was crucified between two robbers, one on his right and one on his left. All those who saw him mocked him, though Luke does record that one robber changed his mind, saying, "Jesus, remember me when you come into your kingdom," with Jesus responding, "Truly I tell you, today you will be with me in paradise" (Luke 23:42–43).

Jesus – no doubt weakened by the whipping he had received – only took hours to die. Normally the soldiers would have broken the legs of the victims to speed up their death, but in Jesus' case it wasn't necessary. Jesus spoke his final words, "It is finished," and gave up his spirit.

This is thought to be the location of Golgotha, the site of Jesus' crucifixion

OLD TESTAMENT FULFILMENT

John 19 records the fulfilment of multiple Old Testament patterns and prophecies as Jesus died. The soldiers cast lots for his clothing (Psalm 22:18). Not one of Jesus' bones was broken (Psalm 34:20). The people looked upon "the one they had pierced" (Zechariah 12:10).

King of the Jews

The trials and crucifixion of Jesus are full of kingly language. Jesus was dressed in kingly robes, given a crown of thorns, and the soldiers bowed down to him as a way of mocking him. As he died, the charge sheet nailed to the cross above him even read, "King of the Jews" (John 19:19). They did this because they thought no one could look less like a king than Jesus did as he died. Yet the great irony is that Jesus was demonstrating exactly what sort of king he was. He was a king who would exercise his rule by laying his life down for others. Jesus' seeming defeat was in fact his greatest victory, and the cross was Jesus' throne.

Crucifixion by Sadao Watanabe

The meaning of Jesus' death

Matthew 27 records four events that shed light on the meaning of Jesus' death:

Darkness came over the whole land from midday until 3 p.m. Darkness was a sign of God's judgment, and Amos had even promised that when God came in judgment, the sky would go dark at noon (Amos 8:9). This darkness was a sign that Jesus was suffering God's judgment, in the place of his people.

Jesus cried out, "My God, my God, why have you forsaken me?", which is a quotation from Psalm 22. On the cross, Jesus was separated from and forsaken by his Father – something so unthinkable that it would have been far worse than the physical pain he endured. Like the scapegoat of Leviticus 16, Jesus had left the city. Like Adam, Jesus had been cast out because of sin – though unlike Adam, not for his own sin, but his people's. He was suffering the punishment of exclusion from God that humanity's sin deserved.

The Temple curtain was torn in two from top to bottom. This curtain had symbolized humanity's exclusion from the presence of God. Just as Eden had been guarded by cherubim after Adam had been cast out, so the Temple curtain was embroidered with huge cherubim, showing the way back to God had not yet been opened. As Jesus died, the Temple curtain was torn in two from top to bottom, showing that a way had been made for humanity to return to Eden, to return to the presence and blessing of God. Jesus was cast out of God's presence, so his people could enter in.

The dead came to life. Isaiah had promised that when things were made new, the tombs would split and the dead would be raised (Isaiah 26:19), and this happened as Jesus died. This pointed to the life that was made possible through Jesus' death. He died, so that his people might live.

Jesus was mocked by being given a crown of thorns

THE RESURRECTION: NEW CREATION BEGUN

The apostle Paul said that if the resurrection didn't happen, the Christian faith was futile (1 Corinthians 15:14). The whole religion stands or falls on it. Although the resurrection would shape the grand tapestry of history, it all begins in the pale light of dawn, with two women. Two of Jesus' friends, both called Mary, walk quickly to the tomb, waves of grief overwhelming them. But then imagine their shock, their disbelief, their *joy* as they are told by an angel that the one they most loved is not dead, but alive...

The empty tomb

After Jesus died, he was laid in a tomb belonging to a rich disciple called Joseph of Arimathea, and a large stone was rolled across the entrance. The tomb was sealed, and a Roman guard set.

On the first day of the week – the third day after Jesus' death – the two women went to the tomb to embalm Jesus' body with spices. Before they got there, there was an earthquake and an angel rolled the stone back from the tomb. "He has risen," said the angel, and showed them the place where Jesus had laid (Matthew 28:6).

OLD TESTAMENT FULFILMENT

Jesus' resurrection is prefigured multiple times in the Old Testament. Jonah was in the fish for three days before being returned to life (Jonah 1:17). Hosea speaks of the nation of Israel as dying and then being raised on the third day (Hosea 6:2). The most explicit reference is Psalm 16: "you will not abandon me to the realm of the dead, nor will you let your faithful one see decay", which the apostle Peter sees as being a prediction of the resurrection of Christ (Acts 2:31).

Resurrection appearances

Just as women had been some of the last ones to remain with Jesus as he died, so it was women who first met him after the resurrection. Mary was the first to see the risen Jesus, but perhaps due to the tears in her eyes, or in the dim light of dawn she didn't recognize him at first and thought him to be the gardener (John 20:15). This is a touching scene of a tender reunion, yet it also tells a bigger story. It happens at dawn. Jesus' resurrection ushers in a new age, an end of darkness. It happens in a garden, with Jesus looking like a gardener. Jesus is a new Adam, in a new creation. This is not just the beginning of a new day, but a new *world*.

Dawn over Jerusalem

The resurrection portrayed in abstract form

Jesus appeared to the disciples

Jesus then appeared to all the disciples that evening, but Thomas was not present, and refused to believe Jesus had really risen (John 20:25). Only when later Jesus appeared to him did he believe, but the name of "doubting Thomas" has stuck, perhaps unfairly. Thomas is actually a picture of how it happened with all the disciples. None of them were expecting him to rise from the dead. It was only the evidence of the empty tomb and seeing Jesus face-to-face that made them believe. Paul records that Jesus appeared to more than 500 people at one time, many of whom were still alive as he was writing (1 Corinthians 15:6).

Risen and ruling

Jesus' resurrection was proof that his work of redemption was complete. Death is the punishment due for sin, but in rising again Jesus showed that that penalty had been fully paid. Jesus had broken the power of Satan, who held the power of death.

But the resurrection is more than just a proof that the cross worked. When Christ rose from the dead, this was his enthronement as the king promised in 2 Samuel 7 and Psalm 2. This is what Paul means when he says Jesus was "appointed the Son of God in power [a kingly title] by his resurrection from the dead" (Romans 1:4). At Jesus' resurrection, he was exalted to the place of highest honour, and given all authority and power to rule (Philippians 2:9–10).

The ascension

Jesus remained with his disciples for forty days after his resurrection, then ascended to heaven in a cloud (Luke 24:51; Acts 1:9).

Open Heaven by Tim Steward

The ascension is often overlooked, but it is significant for two main reasons.

The enduring humanity of Jesus. Jesus rose bodily from the dead, and he ascended bodily into heaven. Christ never stopped having a body; he never stopped being fully human. There is no end date to the incarnation. This means that Jesus is able to continue as a merciful high priest, who knows human frailty and weakness. It also gives great dignity to human bodies, and to physicality. Jesus has a body (albeit a glorified one), and so will his people for all time.

Humanity in the presence of God. When Jesus ascended into heaven, he did so as a man. A man now lives in the presence of God. Jesus is like Moses, ascending Mount Sinai into the presence of God, or Adam returning up the mountain to Eden. Humanity has got back into paradise. Creation purposes are being fulfilled.

47

PENTECOST: GOD SENDS HIS SPIRIT

As the Gospels end, the disciples are still few in number, and scared. They are hardly the bold evangelists who would take the message of Jesus across the known world, and suffer and die for their faith. The event that turned this group of people upside down – indeed perhaps the greatest turning point in history – was Pentecost, the sending of the Holy Spirit.

Speaking many languages

The Gospel of Luke ends with Jesus ascending into heaven, having told his disciples to wait in Jerusalem until the Holy Spirit came upon them with power. The story continues in Luke's second book, called Acts (see p. 137). Ten days later, they were all together, and the sound of a rushing wind came from heaven, filling the entire house they were in. Tongues of fire came and rested on each of them, and they were all filled with the Holy Spirit. They all began speaking in other languages, and the people from many nations in Jerusalem heard them declaring the wonders of the Lord in their own native tongue (Acts 2:1–4).

Today all around the world Christians gather to worship God

This miracle is a kind of reverse of Babel (see p. 22). Sin led to judgment and division, but the coming of the Spirit points to the unity brought by the gospel of Jesus Christ. It is significant that this is a miracle of speaking *different* languages, not of everyone understanding *one* language. Diversity and cultural differences are good things, to be celebrated. Pentecost pictures the new creation where cultural diversity will remain: all cultures of the world will be represented, but these will no longer be a barrier to communication or fellowship.

The last days: The "overlap of the ages"

The apostle Peter explained the events of Pentecost by quoting from the prophet Joel: "In the last days, God says, I will pour out my Spirit on all people" (Acts 2:17). The pouring out of the Spirit at Pentecost was a sign that the "last days" had begun.

The Old Testament expectation of the future was that all of God's promises would be fulfilled simultaneously, when the Messiah came. The New Testament clarifies that all these promises would *begin* to be fulfilled at the first coming of Jesus, but would only be completely fulfilled when Jesus returned at the end of time.

In the "last days", Christians live in the overlap between two ages. Christians belong to the new age that has begun – characterized by forgiveness, new life with God, and the Spirit. They already enjoy the benefits of forgiveness and new life through Christ's death. But Christians still belong to the old age. Not until Christ returns will they be sinless, and free from pain and suffering (see also p. 148).

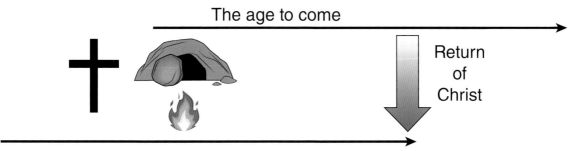

The spirit of Christ

At the Last Supper, Jesus had reassured his fearful disciples that his going away would not be the end. He promised them that he would not leave them as orphans but that he would come to them. He said he would leave them another comforter, the Spirit of truth (John 14:15–18). By this he meant the Holy Spirit. The Holy Spirit is nothing less than the spirit of Christ, who would make Christ present in the hearts of his disciples. Christ could have left his disciples no greater gift. Christ would not be absent, but would be *more* present to his disciples by his Spirit – this is why Jesus could tell his disciples it was *better* that he went away (John 16:7). So it is with Christian believers today: they are closer now to Christ than even the disciples were when Jesus walked the earth (see p. 145, 156).

OLD TESTAMENT FULFILMENT

At the heart of the Bible story is God's promise to dwell amongst his people, to restore the relationship with him that Adam and Eve had lost through their sin. When God had come to dwell amongst his people in the tabernacle and the Temple, this was symbolized by fire filling these two buildings. But when the Temple was rebuilt after the exile, no fire fell. At Pentecost, the fire of God came down again, this time not on a building, but on God's people, individually. No longer would the Temple – or any other building – be a place of meeting with God, but God would dwell within his people. The Spirit is not just given to some believers, or given in stages. Rather, having the Holy Spirit dwell within them is *the* characteristic mark of every Christian believer.

Fire symbolizes the presence of God

Knowledge of God

In the Old Testament, certain figures such as prophets, priests, and kings – even craftsmen – were filled with the Holy Spirit for their ministry, but this was a very limited group. At Pentecost all this changed. Knowledge of God was no longer limited to a particular place, or to a particular group of people. All believers – from the least to the greatest - now know God personally.

Pentecost began the mission of the church, the taking of the good news to all nations (see p. 137). Because the Spirit was poured out on all, all could prophesy – all could declare the good news of what the Lord had done. Jesus' sending of the Spirit is the means by which the promises to Abraham (see p. 23) would be fulfilled – that all the nations of the earth would be blessed in Christ.

ACTS: JESUS' MISSION CONTINUES

The book of Acts is an adventure from start to finish. As the apostles continue the mission of Jesus, there are dangers at every turn: opposition, riots, imprisonments, and a shipwreck. Yet there are also miraculous releases from prison, healings and miracles, and sacrificial generosity within the church community that can only be the work of the Spirit. Thousands come to know God, and the apostles preach with boldness even before the greatest rulers of the day. Acts is a book intended to inspire the church of all ages to join in Jesus' mission.

Philip baptizes the Ethiopian Eunuch by Aelbert Cuyp

To the ends of the earth

At the beginning of Acts, the disciples ask, "Lord, are you at this time going to restore the kingdom to Israel?" (Acts 1:6). Jesus responds: "You will receive power when the Holy Spirit comes on you; and you will be my witnesses in Jerusalem, and in all Judea and Samaria, and to the ends of the earth" (1:8). Jesus was answering point-for-point four misconceptions the disciples had about how Jesus' mission would continue:

QUESTION	JESUS' RESPONSE	EXPLANATION
"Lord, are you…"	"You will receive power."	Jesus will continue his mission, but he will do it through his disciples, as he will be taken up to heaven imminently.
"at this time"	"When the Holy Spirit comes."	The giving of the Spirit is the defining event for the book of Acts; it will set in motion all that follows.
"restore the kingdom"	"You will be my witnesses."	The disciples expected Jesus to restore the kingdom through force and conquest. Jesus sets out an entirely different pattern for kingdom growth: the disciples will be witnesses. They will declare the message of Jesus' life, death, and resurrection.
"to Israel"	"In Jerusalem, in Judea, in and Samaria, and to the ends of the earth."	Jesus broadens their thinking from Israel to the whole earth. The book of Acts is structured by the gospel going out in these concentric circles: Jerusalem (ch. 3–7), Judea and Samaria (ch. 8–9), then the ends of the earth (ch. 10–28).

The gospel going to all nations is not a New Testament innovation: it was always part of God's plan. Adam and Eve were given a task of filling the whole earth (Genesis 1:28). Abraham was promised blessing for *all* nations (Genesis 12:1–3). God has always cared about all nations: "May the peoples praise you, God; may all the peoples praise you" (Psalm 67:3).

Progress reports

Acts records the growth of the church and the spread of the good news about Jesus. The disciples face opposition and obstacles, but each section ends with progress reports, for example "the word of God increased and multiplied" (12:24, ESV, see also 2:47; 6:7; 9:31; 16:5; 19:20). The language used is intentionally echoing the very first command to Adam and Eve: "Be fruitful and multiply" (Genesis 1:28). God's creation plans will be fulfilled. The earth will be filled with "image bearers" who glorify God in all the earth. This happens as the good news of Jesus is taken to the ends of the earth, and people become worshippers of Jesus.

Crossing boundaries

Acts records the crossing of many boundaries. There are geographic boundaries – see p. 140, the map of Paul's journeys around the Mediterranean to preach the good news. But there are also religious boundaries to cross. Peter was given a vision of a sheet coming from heaven with all kinds of animals in it, both clean and unclean, and he was told by God to eat. Peter initially refused but was told, "Do not call anything impure that God has made clean" (Acts 10:15). This was a picture of all foods being declared clean, but *also* of the boundary between Jews and Gentiles being removed, and non-Jews given the same access to God.

Paul in Rome

The book of Acts ends with the apostle Paul being arrested, and taken for trial in Rome. In Rome he is kept under house arrest, while he awaits having his case heard by Caesar. This may seem like an anti-climax, but ultimately the book is not about Paul or any of the apostles. Acts is about the progress of the gospel from Jerusalem to the rest of the world. The good news of Jesus has not reached every people-group on the planet – nor has it 2,000 years later – so in this sense the mission of Acts continues. But by the end of the book, Paul is preaching the gospel in Rome, the heart of the known world. The ending of Acts is meant to inspire confidence that God's mission is progressing, and inspire believers of all succeeding ages to join in this same mission of proclaiming Jesus to every corner of the earth.

PAUL: WITNESS OF THE RESURRECTED CHRIST

The first mention of the apostle Paul (also known as Saul) is when he was one of the onlookers approving the execution of Stephen, a disciple of Christ. Paul was persecuting the church, putting believers in prison, constantly breathing threats and murder. He was a violent, powerful Jewish leader who was committed to attacking the new church. Yet in just one day the direction of his life would change forever.

Paul's vision of the risen Christ

Paul was travelling to Damascus, to arrest Christians and bring them back to Jerusalem. As he was travelling, he suddenly saw a light from heaven, and a voice saying, "Saul, Saul, why do you persecute me?" (Acts 9:4). Paul fell to the ground, blinded. On asking who was speaking, Paul was told that it was Jesus himself. Jesus told Paul to go to the house of a disciple called Ananias in Damascus. Imagine Ananias's shock, as God told him to welcome and pray for this man who had been wanting to kill him. But Ananias did welcome him, and prayed for Paul that his eyes would be opened and he would receive the Holy Spirit. Something like scales fell from Paul's eyes, and he regained his sight. Immediately Paul began teaching that Jesus was the Son of God.

Paul, as a Pharisee, knew the Scriptures very well. But he had not believed that Jesus was who he claimed to be. Things changed when he met the risen and glorified Jesus. Everything else that Paul taught was the outworking of this central realization that Jesus had risen from the dead, and was indeed the Son of God (e.g. 2 Corinthians 5:16–17). Paul became an apostle, and the Lord told Ananias how he would use Paul: "This man is my chosen instrument to proclaim my name to the Gentiles and their kings and to the people of Israel. I will show him how much he must suffer for my name" (Acts 9:15–16).

The Conversion of St Paul by Cristofero di Jacopo

Resurrection and mission

There is a close connection in the Bible between Christ's resurrection and Christian mission. In Matthew's Gospel, immediately after having been raised from the dead, Jesus gave his disciples the "Great Commission" of making disciples of all nations. Their authority to do this comes from Jesus, given all authority when he rose from the dead.

For Paul also, mission flowed naturally out of the fact that Christ had been raised. Paul understood that the age to come had begun with the resurrection of Christ, and that judgment would follow (Acts 17:30–31). Paul realized he was living in the day of salvation. Meeting the risen Jesus spurred him on in his mission of making Christ known in all the world whilst there was still time.

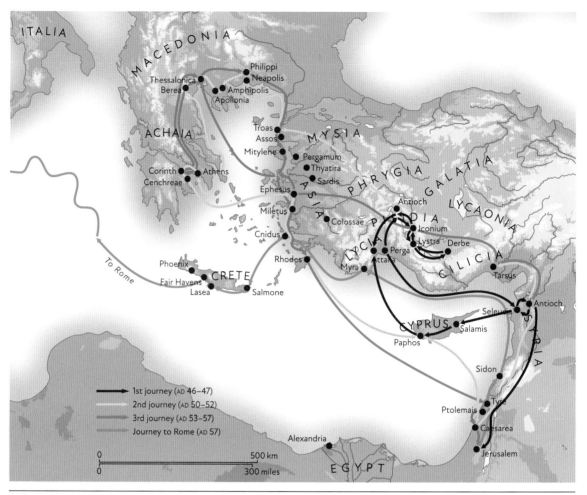

Paul's missionary journeys

Legend:
- 1st journey (AD 46–47)
- 2nd journey (AD 50–52)
- 3rd journey (AD 53–57)
- Journey to Rome (AD 57)

New creation begun

The road to Damascus experience was so transformative for Paul because it showed him where he was in the story. Meeting Jesus, risen and glorified, showed Paul that the new creation *had* begun. God's end time reign had broken into the present. All of the Old Testament prophecies were beginning to be fulfilled in Jesus.

Paul not only understood where he was in the story, but he also saw how the story ended. The story of the Old Testament found its fulfilment in Jesus. Any other way of trying to complete the Old Testament story was wrong. Paul could no longer live as he had done before (Philippians 3:7). He could no longer rely on his Jewish heritage to give him any status before God. He would no longer look to the sacrifices in the Temple to find forgiveness but to Christ. All Paul's theology centres on the risen Jesus Christ.

Major themes in Paul's theology flow from the resurrection of Christ

Justification by faith (p. 142)	Christ's resurrection was his vindication and justification. Since Christians are united to him they receive the same verdict.
Union with Christ (p. 145)	Christ is the resurrected king, the one who fulfils all the promises with God. All the other blessings believers receive are because they are united to *him*.
Christian living (p. 148)	Christians are to live according to their new identity in the risen Christ. They have died to their old selves, and are to set their minds on things above. Many of the struggles in Christian living are about understanding – and living in the light of – the "now and not yet" of these last days.

OLD TESTAMENT FULFILMENT

According to the Old Testament, the new creation began with resurrection. Ezekiel described life being given to a valley of dry bones (Ezekiel 37); Isaiah promised, "Your dead will live, LORD; their bodies will rise" (Isaiah 26:19). Jesus' resurrection was the sign these promises were beginning to be fulfilled. The new age of life – life to the full – had begun with Jesus.

Firstfruits

Paul understood that the resurrection of Christ inaugurated the new age, but that the old age would still continue. He knew that only in the future when Christ returned would his kingdom be fully established and his blessings perfectly enjoyed. Paul describes Christ as the "firstfruits" of the new creation (1 Corinthians 15:20). This is a farming metaphor. We might imagine a woman who owns a vineyard. The first grapes to ripen are brought her to taste – a foretaste of what the rest of the harvest will be like and the guarantee that it is on its way. So too with Christ. His resurrection is a sign of what the future resurrection of all believers will be like. Just as Christ's resurrection body was recognizably still him, yet more glorious, so believers will be given more glorious resurrection bodies for the new creation.

Paul's letters

Paul travelled around the Mediterranean, preaching about Jesus, and planting and strengthening churches. He also wrote letters to churches, many of which are included in the New Testament. When reading Paul's letters it is important to remember they were written to particular people, in particular situations. But Paul – writing under the inspiration of the Holy Spirit – also wrote what churches of all the ages would need to know. The way to read Paul's letters is to ask two questions:

- What did this mean to the original readers?
- What does this mean for us today?

PAUL'S THEOLOGY: JUSTIFICATION BY FAITH

Paul's letter to the Romans has been called the "cathedral of the Christian faith". It inspired Martin Luther to challenge the teaching of the medieval church, and led to the Reformation, a movement that turned Europe upside down in the sixteenth century. At the heart of the book of Romans is the issue which was so important in Martin Luther's time, and indeed in every time. How is humanity to be made right with God? Is it by the good works they do? Or is it simply by having faith?

Saint Paul Writing His Epistles probably by Valentin de Boulogne

Sin

Paul begins by sketching the dark background against which the bright light of the gospel shines. First he speaks of the fact that all human beings are sinful. The fundamental sin is rejection of God. Though all people have some knowledge of God through the world he has made, Paul says that people "suppress the truth" and neither glorify God as God nor give thanks to him (Romans 1:18, 21).

As a result of human sin, "the wrath of God is being revealed from heaven" (1:18). God is rightly angry at human rebellion and wickedness. His wrath is revealed in the present, as he hands people over to their sin, but primarily in the future, on a day when God will justly punish all wickedness.

Neither moral living nor religious observance are enough to escape this sentence. Paul concludes, "There is no one righteous, not even one" (3:10). To be "righteous" is to be in good standing with God, acceptable to him. Paul's damning indictment on all of humanity is that there is no one who is righteous, no one who can stand before God on the day of his judgment.

But now...

Romans 3:21 is one of the great turning points in all of Scripture. The bad news of human sin and God's wrath has been very stark. "But now..." says Paul, and introduces one of the most glorious paragraphs in the Bible.

But now apart from the law the righteousness of God has been made known, to which the Law and the Prophets testify. This righteousness is given through faith in Jesus Christ to all who believe. There is no difference between Jew and Gentile, for all have sinned and fall short of the

glory of God, and all are justified freely by his grace through the redemption that came by Christ Jesus. God presented Christ as a sacrifice of atonement, through the shedding of his blood – to be received by faith.

Romans 3:21–25

Righteousness is available for God's unrighteous people. A way is provided to escape the judgment they deserve. Jesus died as a "sacrifice of atonement" which would wash away sins and deal with God's wrath (3:25). Like the sacrifices of the Old Testament, Jesus died in the place of his people – as a *substitute*. He took the punishment his people deserved (see p. 42 for more on sacrifices).

Justification: The great exchange

The result of Christ's death is that God's people can be *justified*. They can be in the right standing with God, and confident as they face the final judgment day. Being justified involves not simply having one's sins washed away, but also being seen as perfect. Christ fulfilled the law in his people's place, so his righteousness could be counted to them. It is "great exchange" – a swap.

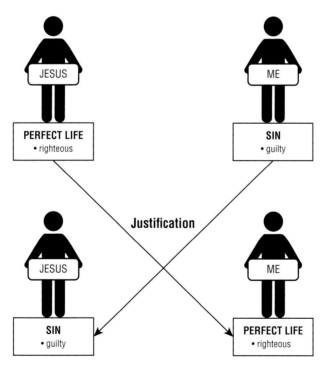

To be "justified" is to have the verdict of the final judgment given in advance – and for that verdict to be "righteous". The result of being justified by faith is that all believers have peace with God (5:1).

Faith not works

Justification is by faith, not by works. A Christian's standing before God is not based on any good deeds that they do. It is simply based on trusting what Christ has done. This is why Christianity is good news. Pharaoh's message was "more bricks!" – constantly demanding more from the people (see p. 31). God rescued his people from this slavery – and from the slavery of any performance-based system. The message of faith, not works, is one of freedom! (Galatians 5:1).

Paul emphasizes that a Christian can never boast. A Christian who is accepted by God can never say, "I've earned this"; rather they must say, "I stand here only because I received a free gift, through Christ's death." This is why arrogance or self-righteousness is such an ugly trait in Christians – because it is in flat contradiction of the central message of Christianity.

OLD TESTAMENT FULFILMENT

The Old Testament always taught that salvation was by faith, not good works. Paul gives the example of the great Jewish hero Abraham: "Abraham believed God and it was credited to him as righteousness" (Romans 4:3; Genesis 15:6). He also quotes King David: "Blessed are those whose transgressions are forgiven, whose sins are covered" (Romans 4:7; Psalm 32:1).

Good works

What about good works? If a Christian is saved by faith, not works, does this mean they are free to live as they like? "By no means!" says Paul (Romans 6:15). Just like the people in Moses' day, who were rescued from slavery and only then given the law, obedience is the right *response* to God's saving work. Jesus didn't die to make obedience unnecessary, he died to make it *possible* (Titus 2:14). But this is not a burdensome thing. Think back to Adam and Eve in the garden. Following God's commands was the way to blessing and life. Their disobedience didn't lead to greater freedom, but to misery. So, too, Christians discover the joy of living God's way; of doing the good works they were created in Christ Jesus to do (Ephesians 2:10).

However, there are two dangers that Christians must beware of:

Legalism	Thinking that their good works or law-keeping are part of earning any merit from God. Paul addresses this very strongly in Galatians.
Lawlessness	Thinking that because they are not saved by good works, God's law can be ignored and they can live as they want. This is the issue that James addresses in his letter (see p. 26).

Justification by faith is a message of freedom in contrast to Pharaoh's call for "more bricks"

PAUL'S THEOLOGY: UNION WITH CHRIST

It might be asked: how can Christ's work 2,000 years ago benefit his people today, so many years later? And how can it be *just* that he should step in and pay for the sins of his people? The answer is found in the doctrine of union with Christ. Over fifty times in his letters Paul refers to Christians being "in Christ" or the equivalent. This is the most fundamental reality for a Christian: that they have been united to Christ by the Holy Spirit, through faith.

"All that I am I give to you"

Union with Christ may initially seem a hard concept to understand, but it is similar to a marriage, where two people become one. In the Anglican marriage service, husband and wife say to each other, "All that I am I give to you, all that I have I share with you."

The first and greatest gift that believers receive from being united to Christ is Christ himself. This is why Paul emphasizes union with Christ so much. For Paul there is no greater joy than knowing God.

"All I have I share with you"

This union with Christ means all that is his, also now belongs to the believer – just as when two people marry their possessions become shared. This is how the great exchange referred to on p. 143 can be possible. This is why human sin can justly be passed to Christ, and his righteousness given to his people. Christ and his people are united together – are *one*.

As John Calvin said, "We must understand that as long as Christ remains outside of us, and we are separated from him, all that he has suffered and done for the salvation of the human

Union with Christ is like a marriage where two become one

Just as Adam and Eve's sin led to condemnation for all their offspring, so Jesus' obedience led to life for all who are united to him (Romans 5:18)

race remains useless and of no value for us... All that he possesses is nothing to us until we grow into one body with him."[11]

Christ as representative

Because Christians are united to Christ, Jesus is their *representative*. What happens to him is seen as happening to all believers. This is similar to in football, where eleven players represent their country – Brazil for example – and when they win, all of Brazil can say "*we won*".

OLD TESTAMENT FULFILMENT

Jesus' representative role is foreshadowed in the Old Testament by the relationship between the king and the people. The fate of the people was tied to the fate of the king. When David defeated Goliath, all God's people shared in the victory (see p. 60). When Manasseh sinned, all God's people suffered the consequence of exile (see p. 81).

But the great representative figure of the Old Testament is *Adam*. He sinned and everyone after him shared in his fate. Christ came as the "second Adam", who succeeded where Adam failed. All humanity is now either "in Adam" – sharing in his death, curse, and exile – or "in Christ" – sharing in his life, blessing, and relationship with God.

United with Christ in his death

Paul says believers have "died with Christ" (Romans 6:8). Because believers are united to Christ, his death 2,000 years ago is not distant from them; rather it is a death they died. It was a death to their old sinful way of life so that they might live for Christ. Christians need fear no future punishment for sin, because in Christ they have already died the death they deserve: "Therefore, there is now no condemnation for those who are in Christ Jesus" (Romans 8:1).

United with Christ in his resurrection

More than that, Christians are united with Christ in his resurrection. In Ephesians, Paul speaks of Jesus being raised from the dead and seated in the heavenly places (Ephesians 1:20). But then in the next chapter he uses almost identical language to speak of what has happened to believers: "God raised us up *with Christ* and seated us *with him* in the heavenly realms *in Christ Jesus*" (Ephesians 2:6, emphasis added).

Paul is not speaking about Christians physically having gone to heaven; he is speaking about *spiritual* realities:

- Christ has conquered death and so have all who are united to him.
- Christ has been accepted by God and so have all who are united to him.
- Christ has been seated in God's presence and so have all who are united to him.

Implications of being "raised with Christ"

- **Assurance.** A Christian's fundamental identity is not found in him or herself. It is found in Christ. A Christian could not be more accepted, or closer to God than they already are, because they are as accepted and as close to God as Christ is. This is why all believers – both male and female – are described as having been adopted as "sons" (Galatians 3:26). It is because they now have the same privileges and access to God as Christ *the* Son has. One of the chief of these is free access to God in prayer: the privilege of calling him "Father".

- **Holiness.** Christians are those who have been given a new identity, and they are called to live in light of it: "Since, then, you have been raised with Christ, set your hearts on things above, where Christ is" (Colossians 3:1). The new life Christians have been given is for the sake of living for God.

Salt and Light by Tim Steward

Just as Adam was created to do good works, to fill the earth with the glory of God, so Christians are those who have been "re-created" for good works, which God prepared in advance for them to do (Ephesians 2:10). Christians are now able to fulfil the original command given to Adam and Eve, and make God known in all the earth.

CHRISTIAN LIVING IN THE LAST DAYS: TENSION

Christians live in the "overlap of the ages" (see p. 135). They live between two worlds, with all the tension and conflict this implies. They have received some of the benefits of salvation, but await the return of Christ for other blessings to be fully realized. What is life like in this "now and not yet" situation?

"Both righteous and a sinner" was a key teaching of Martin Luther the German Reformer in the sixteenth century. Portrait by Lucas Cranach

Both righteous and a sinner

When someone comes to Christ, their sins are immediately forgiven and Christ's righteousness is credited to them. This is a once-for-all declaration: a Christian is righteous and forgiven, and this status does not depend on their behaviour or progress in the faith. But the New Testament is clear that Christians will continue to sin, right up until Christ returns. There is battle between their old nature and the Spirit at work within them. Now they are Christians, they have the desire and ability to fight sin and pursue godliness (Romans 13:14). This growth in holiness is often known as "sanctification", which is a process that continues all through a Christian's life. The call to holiness is not a burdensome thing. Christians have been united with Christ, they have been raised with Christ, they have been made holy in God's sight. The call to grow in holiness is simply a call to be in practice what in status they already are.

"Christ being formed in you"

Adam and Eve were created in the image of God, to be like him and to represent him to the world. But their sin meant that they were no longer like God as they should have been – and this is the same for all humanity since. Christ, as the sinless perfect man, was the true image of God. As Christians contemplate him, they too are "transformed into his image with ever-increasing glory" (2 Corinthians 3:18). By beholding Christ, Christians become more like him, and indeed become more like they were always intended to be. Growth in holiness is not about conformity to a set of abstract rules, but about becoming more like Christ, or as Paul writes to the Galatians, about Christ being "formed in you" (Galatians 4:19).

Relationship with the world

Christians no longer feel at home in the world. They have a new allegiance, and live differently to those around them. Being a Christian will be hard. Jesus said to his disciples that they no

Jesus describes Christian living as being on a steep, narrow path, which can be hard at times, but which has a glorious destination

longer belong to the world, and so will be hated, just as he himself was hated first (John 15:18–19). The majority of Jesus' apostles, and many Christians throughout church history, lost their lives because they refused to renounce Jesus. Jesus says this is not a surprise: after all, he himself was killed by his opponents.

A Christian's relationship with the world is not simply one of suffering. Christians are witnesses of Christ, testifying to his death and his resurrection. Though at times this message will seem very weak, Paul says, "I am not ashamed of the gospel, because it is the power of God that brings salvation to everyone who believes" (Romans 1:16).

Sorrowful yet always rejoicing

Just as Jesus entrusted himself to God, who judges justly, so Christians who suffer for their faith are not to retaliate, or to return evil for evil. They are to look to the example of Jesus, who "for the joy set before him endured the cross, scorning its shame, and sat down at the right hand of God" (Hebrews 12:2). It is only the sure and certain hope of resurrection that enables Christians to lay their lives down for Christ in this life.

Yet there is great joy in the Christian life *now*, primarily through the ministry of the Holy Spirit. Christians know God as Father, who directs all things for their good (Romans 8:28), and loves to hear their prayers. Christians know peace with God and have a sure hope of heaven.

OLD TESTAMENT FULFILMENT

In Romans 8, which speaks of the tensions of Christian living, Paul quotes from Psalm 44 to explain Christian experience. The psalms portray with great realism the tension of living in this world as a believer: great joys, wonderful relationship, and security with God, but also trials and persecutions – just as Jesus himself experienced.

Understanding God's timing

One of the most important issues when interpreting the Bible is understanding God's timing. The Old Testament is full of extraordinary promises of material blessing and prosperity for God's people. The New Testament does not diminish these, but *adds* to them. But it can be disastrous for Christians if they do not know *when* they can expect to experience these blessings. Many blessings are enjoyed now, but some will only be fully experienced in the new creation when Christ returns. Wrong expectations can lead to great disappointment and the feeling either that God has let the person down or that they don't themselves have enough faith.

CHRISTIAN EXPERIENCE IN THE PRESENT	
Security	Forgiven, justified, adopted as God's sons, joy in the spirit.
Inclusion	Part of a worldwide family that unites people across social and ethnic barriers (Ephesians 2:11–20).
Provision	Not perfect health and wealth, but God promises to meet all his children's needs (Matthew 6:33).
Perseverance	Living by faith not by sight, with a certain hope of bodily resurrection.
Change	Growing in holiness by the Spirit's power, though not perfect in this life.
Tension	Still suffering in this fallen world, but God working all things for good (Romans 8:28).
Purpose	Living the kingdom life and making Christ known among the nations.

53

THE CHURCH: GOD'S PLAN FOR THE WORLD

Adam and Eve were placed in the paradise Garden of Eden, where they could walk with God and enjoy his presence, but they were not to remain there. Rather they were to go out, filling the earth and subduing it, bringing the rest of the world to the same degree of glory as the garden. In in a similar way, the people of God are not meant to be inward looking, huddled together away from the rest of the world. They are to go out and make God known in all the earth.

Nuns watching a Christmas Eve procession in Bethlehem

From every nation

In the Old Testament, being a member of God's people was primarily about ethnic descent – being in one of the twelve tribes of Israel descended from Abraham. When Jesus chose for himself twelve disciples, he was making the point that being a member of the people of God would no longer be about the family you were born in, but rather about relationship with him: "To all who did receive him, to those who believed in his name, he gave the right to become children of God" (John 1:12). This was always God's plan. Jesus was the promised offspring of Abraham through whom blessing would come to people from every tribe, nation, and language (Genesis 12:1–3).

The church

The word "church" is a word that usually has religious connotations today, but in Bible times it simply meant "gathering" or "assembly". The first "church" was when God's redeemed people gathered to meet with him at Mount Sinai, and hear his word to them. This is a pattern that continues into the New Testament: a Christian church is a community gathered around Christ to hear his word. There are many buildings today that we call "churches" – many of them exquisitely beautiful, and great blessings to the groups that meet there. But biblically speaking, the word "church" always refers to *people*, not to bricks and mortar.

OLD TESTAMENT FULFILMENT

Peter describes the church in terms rich with Old Testament imagery: "You are a chosen people, a royal priesthood, a holy nation, God's special possession, that you may declare the praises of him who called you out of darkness into his wonderful light" (1 Peter 2:9). It is through the church that God will bring to completion all his Old Testament promises.

One heavenly gathering: The universal church

"Church" can refer to believers gathered around Christ in heaven. Believers have been raised with Christ, and so are already part of this spiritual gathering in heaven, even while they still live on earth. So all Christians all round the world and through time are part of that one universal church. This heavenly or universal church is made up of all who have faith in Christ, and so have been united to him through baptism with the Holy Spirit.

The church is described as the bride of Christ

Local gatherings: The local church

"Church" can also refer to a local gathering: the church of Christ in Colossae, or wherever. Local churches are not just small pieces of the larger church. Rather they are representations of the whole. As one author put it, when you look up in the sky and see a crescent moon, you don't say, "There's *part* of the moon", you say, "There's the moon."[12] The local church should be a picture of the heavenly gathering.

This is one reason why churches should be people of a mixture of ages, backgrounds, ethnicities, and abilities. The church is to be a visual aid of God's reconciling power. As groups of people who are very different are reconciled and united in the church, this is a picture of God's power to reconcile humanity to himself (Ephesians 3:8–11). The church is God's means of fulfilling his original commands to Adam, and of the promise to Abraham of blessing for all nations.

Metaphors for the church

Body (1 Corinthians 12, Ephesians 4)	All members are equally important and need each other. All have gifts necessary for the building up of the body. Christ is the head of the body, and the body can only be healthy if it remains connected to him.
Bride (Ephesians 5:22–32)	Christ is the bridegroom, and the church is his bride. This image speaks of the intense love and delight Christ has for his people, and their corresponding call to be holy and pure for him.
Building (Ephesians 2:19–22; 1 Peter 2:4–5)	In the Old Testament, God dwelled on earth in the Temple. Now he dwells amongst his people, the church. God's people are a building, or temple, built on the foundation of the scriptures, and growing as the Scriptures are taught.

When a church gathers

Old Testament believers used to hold their assemblies on the sabbath – the seventh day of the week. But from the start, Christians gathered to meet on the first day of the week – Sunday – to commemorate that as the day when Jesus rose from the dead.

Christian gatherings look very different in different parts of the world, with different languages and cultures expressed. But there are certain common elements which date right back to the book of Acts. There is a "vertical" dimension to what happens when churches meet. Christians gather in God's presence to worship him. They hear God speak through his word, celebrate his death through the Lord's Supper, and respond in prayer and song. But there is also a "horizontal" dimension: encouraging one another and using gifts to build one another up. This gathering on Sunday should shape the rest of the life together in community, as the people care for one another as part of one body. Churches are a foretaste of the new creation, when God's people from every tribe and language will join around the throne of Jesus Christ, singing his praise.

Singing has always been a central part of Christians gathering together to worship

FATHER, SON, AND SPIRIT: THE TRINITY

The "last days" which began at Pentecost may rightly be called the "age of the Spirit". But who is the Holy Spirit? And how does he relate to Jesus and to God the Father? What about Jesus himself? Thomas called him "My Lord and my God", but how does this fit with the fundamental Jewish belief that there is only *one* God? These were some of the questions the first Christians wrestled with. Though the term didn't exist yet, they were considering the doctrine of the *Trinity*.

One God in three persons

The Old Testament clearly affirmed that there is one God (Deuteronomy 6:4). This was central to Jewish faith: it was a *monotheistic* religion. It would have been unthinkable, therefore, for the apostles to add to the number of Gods by saying that Jesus and the Holy Spirit were also separate gods. New Testament writers, like the Old Testament believers, affirm that there is only one God (James 2:19).

The church council of Nicea gathered to affirm the full divinity of Jesus resulting in the Nicene creed that Christians still recite today. This depiction is by Theophanes the Cretan from Stavronikita monastery, Mount Athos

Yet from the very beginning, Jesus was seen as divine (see p. 108). He did what only God could do: he accepted worship, and he called God his Father, making himself equal with God (John 5:18). Rather than being a rival God, Jesus could say, "I and the Father are one" (John 10:30).

The Holy Spirit was likewise seen as divine right from the start: in Acts, when Ananias and Sapphira lied to the Holy Spirit, Peter told them, "You have not lied just to human beings but to God" (Acts 5:4).

There is one God, but that God exists as Father, Son, and Holy Spirit in perfect loving relationship. There can be no division between Father, Son, and Spirit; in every action they are all involved, even if they may have different roles. Later Christians would clarify the language to speak of one God, in three persons. The word "Trinity" points to the threeness and the oneness of God.

OLD TESTAMENT FULFILMENT

The key Old Testament belief is that there is one God (Deuteronomy 6:4). But even in the Old Testament there are hints of plurality within God. The New Testament does not correct Old Testament views of God, but extends it. One writer gives the analogy of turning up the lights in a room – no furniture is added, but what was only seen dimly is now seen more clearly.[13]

Fire – representing the holiness of the Spirit; dove representing the peace that the Holy Spirit brings depicted in a stained-glass window in St Peter's Basilica in Vatican City

The God who is Trinity

No analogy or picture can capture what it is for God to be Trinity; they all fail at crucial points. The doctrine of the Trinity points to a God who is utterly beyond human comprehension: a God who is vast and mysterious and *unlike* human beings. The right response is not to try to draw a picture, but to fall down in worship.

The doctrine of the Trinity also shows that the God of the Bible is unlike the god of any other religion. At the very heart of who God is, he is Father, Son, and Spirit in perfect relationship. God is love. God didn't create the world because he was lonely, or lacking anything. Rather he is and always has been a blaze of perfect love, joy, and fellowship between Father, Son, and Spirit. The creation of the world is an overflow of this love. The very goal of the whole Bible story is that human beings can be brought into this relationship of love.

The Holy Spirit

The Holy Spirit is the third person of the Trinity: not an impersonal force, but God himself, who with the Father and the Son is to be worshipped and glorified.

The gift of the Spirit to all believers is their greatest blessing in this life, as he is the firstfruits of the age to come, and the guarantee of their future redemption. He is given different titles in the New Testament which point to his work.

Spirit of truth (John 14:17)	The Holy Spirit ensured the disciples remembered accurately about Jesus, and caused the New Testament to be written. He still speaks today through the Scriptures, and enables believers to understand God's word. Moreover, he enables and motivates believers to speak of Christ in mission, just as happened with the apostles at Pentecost.
Spirit of life (Romans 8:2)	New life is given by the Spirit – only through the Spirit's work can people be "born again" and come to know Christ. The new life of believers is also characterized by the Spirit, as they are led by him and, through him, know God personally.
Spirit of holiness (Romans 1:4)	The work of the Spirit in believers is to make them more like Jesus. The "fruit of the Spirit" that he causes to develop in believers is nothing less than the character of Christ being formed in them: "love, joy, peace, forbearance, kindness, goodness, faithfulness, gentleness and self-control" (Galatians 5:22–23).
The gifts of the Spirit (1 Corinthians 12, Romans 12)	The Spirit gives gifts, to enable believers to serve one another for the building up of the church. Some are more "supernatural": healing, miracles, speaking in tongues. Others are more "normal": hospitality, administration, giving. These gifts are to be exercised in love, not in a self-seeking way.
Spirit of Christ (Romans 8:9)	The Holy Spirit unites believers to Christ, giving believers the rights and privileges of sons. The Spirit prays for believers, testifies to them of God's love, and points believers to Christ. See also p. 134.

THE RETURN OF CHRIST: THE DAY OF JUSTICE

Will justice prevail in the end? Will wrongs one day be righted? Is there a final reckoning for tyrants and abusers? Phrased like this, most people instinctively want a final judgment where those who have escaped all justice in this life will one day face up for their crimes. The Bible teaches that such a day of judgment is coming. This is good news. But it is also sobering, because Jesus says that evil is not simply "out there". It is something that all of us know in our own hearts.

Many artists have painted the final judgment, but even the greatest pieces of art can't fully capture the solemnity, majesty, and gravity of what Scripture describes. This version by Leopold Kupelwieser is in the Altlerchenfelder church in Vienna

Return of Christ to judge

The apostle Paul, when speaking to philosophers in Athens, said that the next big event in human history – the one thing they must come to terms with – would be the return of Jesus Christ (Acts 17:31). When Christ returns it will be with trumpet blast, in great splendour and glory. Earth and heaven will flee away, and all the dead will be raised. Everyone who has ever lived will stand before the judgment seat of Christ. All will be asked to give an account before Christ of how they have lived. The whole Bible has taught that no one could stand on their own merit on that day. Some people have lived better lives than others, but all have sinned and fallen short of the glory of God (Romans 3:23).

Hell and condemnation

Repeatedly in Scripture, God's punishment for sin has been casting people out of his presence and away from his goodness. All the judgments in Scripture have been foreshadowings of the great and final judgment. This place of separation from God and all his goodness is called "hell". Jesus spoke of hell more than anyone else and described it as a place of eternal punishment and anguish, a place "where the fire never goes out" (Mark 9:43). Jesus loved people enough to be honest about where rebellion against God would lead, and told them how to be saved. This is why he spent far more of his time preaching than healing: "I take no pleasure in the death of anyone, declares the Sovereign Lord. Repent and live!" (Ezekiel 18:32).

OLD TESTAMENT FULFILMENT

The many occasions in the Old Testament where God intervened to judge wickedness – the flood in Noah's day, the destruction of Jerusalem by the Babylonians – are all sobering pictures of the judgment to come at the end of time (2 Peter 3:5–7).

Salvation by grace

Judgment day is inescapable, but the whole Bible has pointed toward how this final judgment can be survived. In the Old Testament, sacrificial animals died in the place of the sinner. This pointed to Jesus, who was the true "lamb of God" who was killed in the place of his people.

This is so different to what many people think – that people get into heaven by doing good deeds. The author C. S. Lewis is reported to have said that the difference between Christianity and all other religions could be summarized in one word: *grace*. Every other religion gives things that people have to *do* to gain acceptance and blessing. Christianity speaks of what Christ has *done*, which is a free gift to all who trust in him, a gift of *grace* (Ephesians 2:8).

Two options

There are only two options when it comes to judgment day, and these are beautifully pictured by two buildings on London's skyline. The first option is to plead one's own good deeds. This can be visualized by the statue of Lady Justice on top of the Old Bailey, with her scales of justice. Hope that one's good deeds outweigh the bad and so the sword of judgment won't fall. Yet the sin of rejection of God is so weighty that no good deeds could make up for this.

The second option is to ask for mercy. Above the statue of Lady Justice may be seen the Golden Cross atop St Paul's Cathedral. The cross also is a place of justice. But it is a place of mercy, where the sword of justice fell on Jesus Christ, so that his people could receive life.

When will Christ return?

No one knows when Christ will return. Many of Jesus' parables warn of the unexpected nature of his coming, and that no one can predict it. Rather than encouraging speculation, Jesus rather tells his followers to be ready (Matthew 24:36–44).

The London skyline with Lady Justice on the Old Bailey and St Paul's Cathedral

What are the events leading up to Christ's return? There are three main views on this which depend on when Christ's return is in relation to the thousand years ("millennium") spoken of in Revelation 20.

Premillennialism	Jesus will return before the millennium. On this view, the millennium is a 1,000-year reign of Christ on earth, a time of peace and prosperity for believers when many Old Testament prophecies are fulfilled.
Postmillennialism	Jesus will return after the millennium. This view has an optimistic view of history, with the world gradually becoming more and more Christian, culminating in a "golden age" just before Christ returns. On this view, Christ's return is most likely still some way off in the future.
Amillennialism	On this view, there is no distinct millennium; it simply refers to the entire church age. On this view, the return of Christ is usually seen as imminent – "It could be today."

THE END OF ALL THINGS: THE NEW CREATION

Happy endings are enduringly popular in stories and films. We are hard-wired to want things to turn out well. More than that, we want the end of the story to really match the beginning. The Bible concludes with a vision of the future in which Christ is triumphant, evil is defeated, and all God's creation plans and promises have been fulfilled. It is a wedding, a feast, a riot of celebration, to be enjoyed all the more because of the astonishing journey it took to get there. If you made this story up, no one would believe you...

John of Patmos watches the descent of New Jerusalem from God in a fourteenth-century tapestry

The book of Revelation

The book of Revelation is the apostle John's vision of heavenly and future realities, which he received when in exile on the Isle of Patmos. The vision was to encourage him and other suffering Christians by giving them a picture of where history was heading. Though the vision is complex, at the centre is a throne, with God sitting on it, guiding history. Christians need to understand the story: where history is going and who is in charge.

Defeat of Satan

The early chapters of Revelation describe the sufferings and tribulations of God's people. Satan, represented by a beast and a dragon, is persecuting the church. But as Revelation draws to a close, Satan is thrown into the lake of fire (Revelation 20:10). There is no grand final battle in the book. Christ has crushed the serpent's head and thrown him out of the garden, never to return (see p. 20).

Eden perfected

The final two chapters of the Bible describe the new heavens and the new earth. The language is that of Eden: gold, jewels, the tree of life, a river flowing out. But this is not simply a return to Eden – it is so much *better* than Eden.

The new Jerusalem is a perfect cube – the shape of the Holy of Holies in the Temple. Now the whole *world* has become a dwelling place for God, with Christ, the last Adam, reigning in glory.

This is what creation was always supposed to have become. This is Eden perfected and glorified. Every promise God has made has been fulfilled. God once more dwells with his people, and all that might hurt them has been removed:

Look! God's dwelling-place is now among the people, and he will dwell with them. They will be his people, and God himself will be with them and be their God. He will wipe every tear from their eyes. There will be no more death or mourning or crying or pain, for the old order of things has passed away.

Revelation 21:3–4

Christ at the centre

At the heart of this vision of the future is Jesus Christ. The whole story of the Bible has been about him. This future described is *his* future. God's people will experience all the riches of the new creation, because when they are united to Christ; his story becomes their story.

In John's vision of heaven he sees the elders, living creatures, and thousands upon thousands of angels praising Jesus:

Worthy is the Lamb, who was slain,
*   to receive power and wealth and wisdom and strength*
*   and honour and glory and praise!*

Revelation 5:12

This song captures one of the reasons the new creation is so much better than Eden. In Eden, God was known as creator and sustainer. By the time the story ends, his character has been more clearly revealed. He has shown his people the depths of his love: he was prepared to suffer and die for them. And for that, they praise him for eternity.

Also, God's people are now not simply *sinless* like Adam and Eve first were, but are *unable* to sin. There is no possibility that things will ever be spoiled by sin, as happened the first time. The reason for this change is that they now know God perfectly: they see Christ face to face.

New creation

This picture is a far cry from the disembodied purely spiritual existence that many assume to be the final destiny of believers. Revelation's picture of the

Painting from the Padre Pio church in San Giovanni Rotondo, Italy, portraying the new creation with Christ the lamb of God at the centre

future is of a *new creation* that will be more physical, more vibrant, more real, and more weighty than our world is now. Believers will not be disembodied spirits, but will have resurrection bodies, like Christ after he rose from the dead.

All that is good about this world will be present in the new creation, but purified and perfected to the glory of God. The new creation will not be a place of passivity, of boredom. It will be a place of vibrancy, of activity, of life.

Images of the future

The language used of new creation is symbolic; not like a high-definition photo, but more like an impressionistic painting, intended to convey what it *feels* like. The new creation is described as a wedding with the church as the bride, deeply loved and treasured by her husband Jesus Christ. It is a feast – a time of community and celebration and the finest of food. It is a city of peace. It is coming home after being in exile. It is light after the darkness. It is the desert now blooming with wildflowers and lush meadows. It is the hills dripping with wine. It is gold and precious stones – all of which reflect the greater beauty of the glory of Jesus Christ. It is thousands upon thousands of angels in joyful assembly. It is multitudes from every nation and language, together praising God in perfect bliss, singing, "Salvation belongs to our God, who sits on the throne, and to the Lamb" (Revelation 7:10).

As the book closes, Jesus speaks words to comfort his disciples: "Yes, I am coming soon."

Amen. Come, Lord Jesus.

The Tree of Life - stained-glass window by Roger Wagner in St Mary's Church, Iffley

NOTES

1. David Biema, "The Case for Teaching the Bible", *TIME* magazine, 22 March 2007.
2. P. Wilby, *We Should All Celebrate the Christian Story, Whether or Not We are Believers*, New Statesman: https://www.newstatesman.com/politics/uk/2015/12/we-should-all-celebrate-christian-story-whether-or-not-we-are-believers (last accessed 1 June 2020).
3. Jonty Rhodes, *Covenants Made Simple: Understanding God's Unfolding Promises to His People* (Phillipsburg, NJ: P&R, 2013), p. 21.
4. Peter J. Gentry and Stephen J. Wellum, *Kingdom Through Covenant: A Biblical–Theological Understanding of the Covenants* (Wheaton: Crossway, 2012), p. 170.
5. The phrase 'salvation through judgment' is taken from the title of James M. Hamilton's excellent book *God's Glory in Salvation Through Judgment: A Biblical Theology* (Wheaton, IL: Crossway, 2010).
6. John R. W. Stott, *Understanding the Bible* (revised edition; London: Scripture Union, 1984), p. 51.
7. L. Michael Morales, *Who Shall Ascend the Mountain of the Lord? A Biblical Theology of the Book of Leviticus* (Nottingham: Apollos, 2015), p. 21.
8. Derek Kidner, *Proverbs*, Tyndale Old Testament Commentary (Westmont, IL: IVP, 1964), p. 35.
9. G. K. Beale, *The Temple and the Church's Mission: A Biblical Theology of the Dwelling Place of God* (Nottingham/Westmont: Apollos/IVP, 2004), pp. 352–53.
10. Miroslav Volf, *Exclusion and Embrace* (Nashville, TN: Abingdon Press, 1996), p. 223.
11. John Calvin, *Institutes of the Christian Religion*, III.i.1.
12. Alec Motyer, *Isaiah by the Day: A New Devotional Translation* (Tain, UK: Christian Focus, 2011), p. 306.
13. Benjamin B. Warfield, "The Biblical Doctrine of the Trinity", in *The Works of Benjamin B. Warfield*, vol. 2: *Biblical Doctrines* (New York: Oxford University Press, 1932; reprint, Grand Rapids, MI: Baker, 2003), pp. 14–142.

GLOSSARY

Abraham (also known as Abram). The father of God's Old Testament people. God's promises to Abraham in Genesis 12:1–3 set the rest of the story of the Old Testament in motion.

Apostle This word meaning "messenger" is used for Jesus' twelve disciples (and later Paul) who Jesus authorized to be his witnesses and to pass on his message.

Ark of the Covenant This throne-like chest contained the two tablets of stone on which God wrote the Ten Commandments. The Ark of the Covenant was placed at the heart of the tabernacle/Temple, as a symbol of God's dwelling among his people.

Ascension Forty days after Jesus' resurrection, he ascended into heaven. Christians believe not just that Jesus rose from the dead, but that he is still alive today, and one day will return.

Atonement This refers to the results of sacrifice: sins being covered or washed away, and good relationship with God restored.

Baptism This is a washing with water, symbolizing cleansing and new life. It points to the greater cleansing and new life that Jesus gives internally by his spirit to all who trust in him.

Christ The Greek equivalent of the Hebrew "Messiah" – both of which mean "anointed king". "Christ" is not Jesus' surname, it rather is a description of him as the king promised in the Old Testament, in the line of King David.

Church A word originally meaning "assembly" which is used to refer to God's people – either all God's people everywhere, or a local gathering.

Covenant A formalized relationship, often sealed in blood. When God makes covenants with his people, there are terms for them to keep, with blessings if they keep them, and punishments if they don't.

Cross The Roman means of execution on which Jesus was executed, taking the punishment for the sins of his people.

Curse The opposite of blessing. It is very similar to the word "punishment".

David The great king of Israel, to whom God promised a descendant who would rule forever (2 Samuel 7).

Eden The paradise garden where Adam and Eve dwelt with God when he created the world. When Adam and Eve sinned they were cast out of Eden, and the rest of the Bible is about God's plan not just to restore humankind to Eden, but to bring to perfection all his original purposes in creation.

Evangelism Telling people the good news (gospel) about Jesus Christ. At times this is a synonym with the word "mission".

Exile God punished people for their sin by sending them out of their Promised Land and into exile in Babylon. Exile becomes a symbol of God's people being sent far away from God.

Exodus The great event of deliverance in the Old Testament when God brought his people out of slavery in Egypt to a glorious inheritance, through the shed blood of the Passover lamb. This pattern repeats through Scripture, culminating in the deliverance Jesus (the true Passover lamb) achieved when he brought his people out of slavery to sin through his death on the cross.

Faith Committed, personal trust in God's promises – in particular, the promise to forgive the sins of all who rely on Jesus' death in their place.

Fall The word used to describe Adam's sin, and the effect this had on the world and all humanity afterwards (Genesis 3).

Gentile Someone who is not Jewish. In the Old Testament, Gentiles were not part of the people of God, it was only those descended from Abraham (apart from some exceptions).

Gospel A word meaning "good news". The "gospel" is the message that Jesus Christ is Lord, and that he died for the sins of his people, and rose again to reign. The "gospel" is the summary of the Christian message.

Grace A word describing God's generosity. To be saved by grace is to be saved not based on any good works one does, but rather by God's free gift. Grace is often set in opposition to "works", which tends to refer to systems of merit.

High places Places of illicit worship in Israel and Judah. They were also often places of sexual immorality.

Idol/Idolatry An idol is either an image of God, or a thing that is worshipped in the place of God. One of the repeated sins of God's Old Testament people is that they turned to idolatry – worship of false gods.

Incarnation Refers to God taking human nature and being born as the man Jesus. It comes from the Latin "in carne" meaning "in flesh".

Israel Another name for Jacob, Abraham's grandson. Israel had twelve sons, who became the twelve tribes of Israel, with the name Israel being used for the whole nation. After the kingdom split in King Solomon's day, the northern kingdom kept the name Israel, whilst the southern kingdom became known as Judah.

Jew In the Bible, this word refers to anyone who is a descendant of Abraham, that is the children of Israel. The name "Jew" originates from the Judah tribe.

Just/Justification/Justified The English words "just" and "righteous" both mean to be acceptable in God's sight. To be justified is to be declared acceptable to God. The Bible teaches that justification – being made acceptable to God – is by faith in Jesus, not by any good works that someone does.

Law This word has a broad meaning, usually referring to God's good instructions he gave his people at Mount Sinai, sometimes referring more narrowly to the Ten Commandments and the moral aspects of the instruction God gave.

Messiah See "Christ".

Mission See "Evangelism".

Moses The leader God appointed to bring his people out of slavery in Egypt. One of the great heroes of the Old Testament.

Mount Sinai The mountain in the desert where God's people met with him and received the law after being delivered from Egypt.

Offspring of the serpent/of the woman Refers to the promise in Genesis 3:15. God promises that the offspring of the serpent will strike at the heel of the offspring of the woman, but the offspring of the woman will crush his head. "Offspring of the serpent" figures are those who align themselves with the serpent (Satan) and attack God's people. Jesus is the final "offspring of the woman", who is wounded by the serpent, but ultimately crushes its head and defeats evil forever.

Parable A simple story from everyday life, which Jesus often used to explain or illustrate aspects of his kingdom.

Passover When God delivered his people from slavery at the exodus, he sent judgment on all the land of Egypt: the death of every firstborn son. God's people were told to sacrifice a lamb and daub the blood on the doorposts of their house so that when judgment came, their house would be "passed over" and the son would be spared

Pentateuch The first five books of the Bible, also known as the books of Moses.

Prophet Prophets were those appointed by God to speak his words to the people. When they spoke, they spoke with the authority of God himself.

Repentance Turning away from sin and turning to God. The word indicates a 180-degree change of direction. Repentance and faith are bound together as the necessary and inseparable responses to the good news about Jesus.

Righteous – See "Just".

Sabbath The seventh day of the week which was to be a day of rest. The sabbath was the day of worship in Israel.

Sacrifice In the Old Testament sacrificial system, animals died in the place of people, to pay for their sins. This was a pattern culminating in the death of Jesus. Jesus died as the full and final sacrifice for his people's sins, taking the punishment they deserved.

Satan A powerful angel who rebelled against God. He is the enemy and accuser of God's people throughout the Bible, from when he appears in Genesis 3 in the form of a serpent, to when he is finally thrown into the lake of fire in Revelation 20.

Serpent A serpent appeared in the Garden of Eden as a representation of Satan. Serpents in the Bible usually have this negative connotation.

Sin Rebellion against God and turning away from him. In the Bible, sin is not merely breaking laws (though it includes that) but also breaking relationship with God (e.g. Jeremiah). Sin is the great problem that needs to be fixed for the story to have a happy ending.

Sovereign A word used to describe God being in control. He alone is Creator, with no rivals, and he is totally free to do as he pleases and carry out his plans. This is a great comfort for Christians – God's sovereignty means that nothing can stop him keeping all his promises.

Tabernacle The movable tent that was the dwelling place of God while the people were in the wilderness on the way to the Promised Land. It was a sort of portable Eden, and a portable Sinai, which allowed God to dwell amongst his people. Once the people reached the Promised Land, the tabernacle was replaced with the Temple, which was the same basic structure, but now a permanent building rather than a tent.

Temple See "Tabernacle".

Trinity The word used to describe God as one being who eternally exists in three persons in perfect relationship: Father, Son, and Spirit.

Union with Christ This describes the covenant reality where Christians are united to Christ by his Spirit through faith, so that all that is his becomes theirs.

Yahweh The name of God that he revealed to Moses when he rescued his people from Egypt. Often rendered "Lᴏʀᴅ" in English translations, it speaks of God as self-existent creator, and of his covenant commitment to his people.

PICTURE CREDITS

Maps and diagrams drawn by Westchester Publishing Services, except for: p. 40, Jonathan Adams; p. 45 © 2011 Ralph F. Wilson (pastor@joyfulheart.com); p. 68 Steve Noon. The diagram on p. 28 is based on an idea by Tim Chester in *From Creation to New Creation*, The Good Book Company, 2003. Used with permission. The covenant diagrams on pp. 16, 27, 39 and 127 are adapted with permission from an original idea by Jonty Rhodes in *Covenants Made Simple: Understanding God's Unfolding Promises to His People* (Phillipsburg, NJ: P&R, 2013)

Unit 1, p. 6 www.BibleLandPictures.com / Alamy Stock Photo. **Unit 2**, p. 8 Johannes Groll/Unsplash; p. 9 Alexander Kondakov / Alamy Stock Photo; p. 10 World History Archive / Alamy Stock Photo. **Unit 3**, p. 11 powerofforever/istock; p. 12 Wojtkowski Cezary / Alamy Stock Photo; p. 13 Iryna Zhezher/shutterstock. **Unit 4**, p. 14 GagliardiPhotography/shutterstock; p. 15 Luca Lorenzelli/shutterstock. **Unit 5**, p. 17 jorisvo/shutterstock; p. 18 (top) Francois Roux/shutterstock; p. 18 (bottom) SuperStock / Alamy Stock Photo. **Unit 6**, p. 19 Sonia Halliday Photo Library / Alamy Stock Photo; p. 20 (left) Copyright © O.L.Mississippi Abbey, Dubuque Iowa; p. 20 (right) Maximilian Buzun / Alamy Stock Photo. **Unit 7**, p. 21© Sonia Halliday Photo Library; p. 22 (top) Barcin/istock; p. 22 (bottom) Bridgeman Images. **Unit 8**, p. 23 © Hanan Isachar. **Unit 9**, p. 25 Jouni Pihlman/shutterstock; p. 26 Lebrecht Music & Arts / Alamy Stock Photo; p. 27 vovashevchuk/istock. **Unit 10**, p. 29 The Stapleton Collection / Bridgeman Images; p. 30 Godong / Alamy Stock Photo. **Unit 11**, p. 31 Shanna Baker/Getty Images; p. 32 Lee Carpenter / Alamy Stock Photo; **Unit 12**, p. 34 stigalenas/istock; p. 35 Historic Images / Alamy Stock Photo; p. 36 © Richard Mcbee / Bridgeman Images. **Unit 13**, p. 37 © Sonia Halliday Photo Library/Jane Taylor; p. 38 Dmitriy Feldman svarshik/shutterstock. **Unit 14**, p. 40 Jonathan Adams. **Unit 15**, p. 42 Renata Sedmakova / Shutterstock; p. 43 aslan ozcan/shutterstock. **Unit 16**, p. 45 Copyright © 2011 Ralph F. Wilson (pastor@joyfulheart.com); p. 47 Charles Stirling (Travel) / Alamy Stock Photo. **Unit 17**, p. 48 Valery Voennyy / Alamy Stock Photo; p. 49 blueenayim/istock. **Unit 18**, p. 51 yoglimogli/istock; p. 52 akg-images / Albatross / Duby Tal. **Unit 19**, p. 54 Whit Richardson / Alamy Stock Photo; p. 56 PAINTING / Alamy Stock Photo. **Unit 20**, p. 57 Archive World / Alamy Stock Photo; p. 58 © Hanan Isachar; p. 59 www.BibleLandPictures.com / Alamy Stock Photo. **Unit 21**, p. 60 Gino Santa Maria/shutterstock; p. 61 History and Art Collection / Alamy Stock Photo; p. 62 akg-images / Bible Land Pictures / Z. Radovan / www.BibleLandPictures. **Unit 22**, p. 63 HadelProductions/istock; p. 64 PixelCatchers/istock; p. 65 Bridgeman Images. **Unit 23**, p. 66 agnieszka-kowalczyk/Unsplash; p. 67 Andrew Hagen/shutterstock; p. 68 Steve Noon. **Unit 24**, p. 69 Efired/shutterstock; p. 70 akg-images / Album; p. 71 PhilipCacka/istock. **Unit 25**, p. 72 Sjo/istock; p. 73 Lanmas / Alamy Stock Photo; p. 74 tonisvisuals/istock. **Unit 26**, p. 76 Blackbeck/istock. **Unit 27**, p. 78 DyziO/shutterstock; p. 79 akg-images / Album. **Unit 28**, p. 80 © Zev Radovan, Jerusalem; p. 81 © Zev Radovan, Jerusalem. **Unit 29**, p. 83 The Picture Art Collection / Alamy Stock Photo; p. 84 robertharding / Alamy Stock Photo. **Unit 30**, p. 85 The Picture Art Collection / Alamy Stock Photo; p. 86 akg-images / euroluftbild.de / Gerhard Launer. **Unit 31**, p. 87 akg-images / Erich Lessing. **Unit 32**, p. 90 akg-images / De Agostini Picture Lib. / C. Sappa; p. 91 © Sonia Halliday Photo Library; p. 92 FG Trade/istock. **Unit 33**, p. 93 Santi Rodriguez/shutterstock; p. 94 Heritage Image Partnership Ltd / Alamy Stock Photo; p. 95